CURSIVE PARADISE

KAUR ALIA AHMED

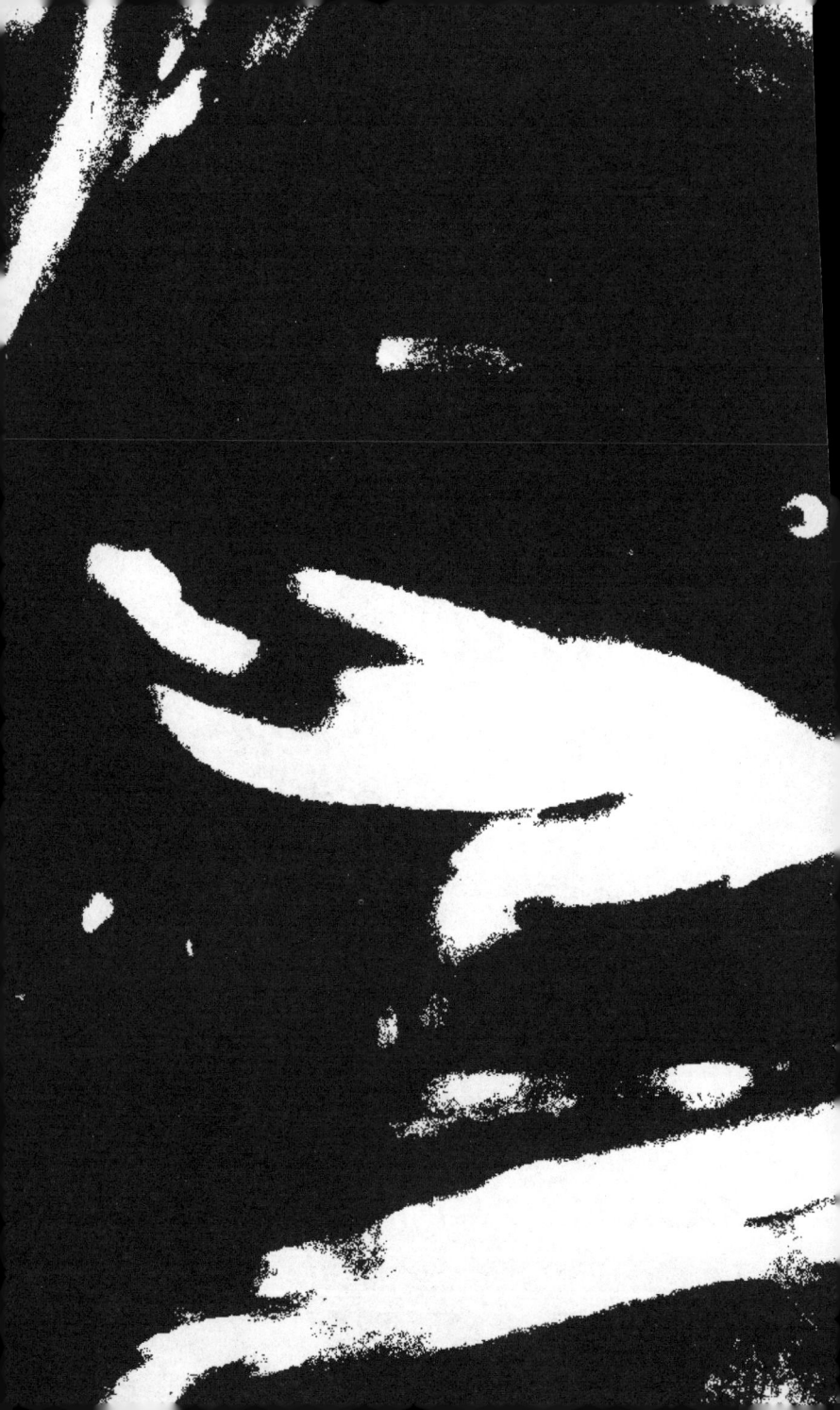

119	find your devastation in the dew drop	
122	razor button	
127	streak the sky	
129	Orange peel here	
130	04/23/2022	7:03AM
133	rhapsodomy	
137	itselfs	
141	copy your spell	
145	gave me nothing to answer	

72	the beige sky my worst fear
76	november three ago
80	drama guarantees it
82	Instamorph
86	print
89	Did not for a moment stop blinking
91	Using my body as my own hammock
95	the heavens a mind, finale
98	Machynis
101	so far as it somehow landed on the same place
109	echo-graphic
112	let the bodies hit the floor
116	defragment

Contents

9	gave me nothing to answer
11	fruit divisions
15	what is love without moisture
24	Piano corpse
29	Umbrella term
32	cutting out pictures of birds
35	in damp posture
42	frame too early
50	low flame
61	imaginary design
63	5:56
67	in verse
69	purr

CURSIVE PARADISE
KAUR ALIA AHMED

WENDY'S SUBWAY

gave me nothing to answer

if truth trips faith
find closure in velcro

play the moment as a freed engraving

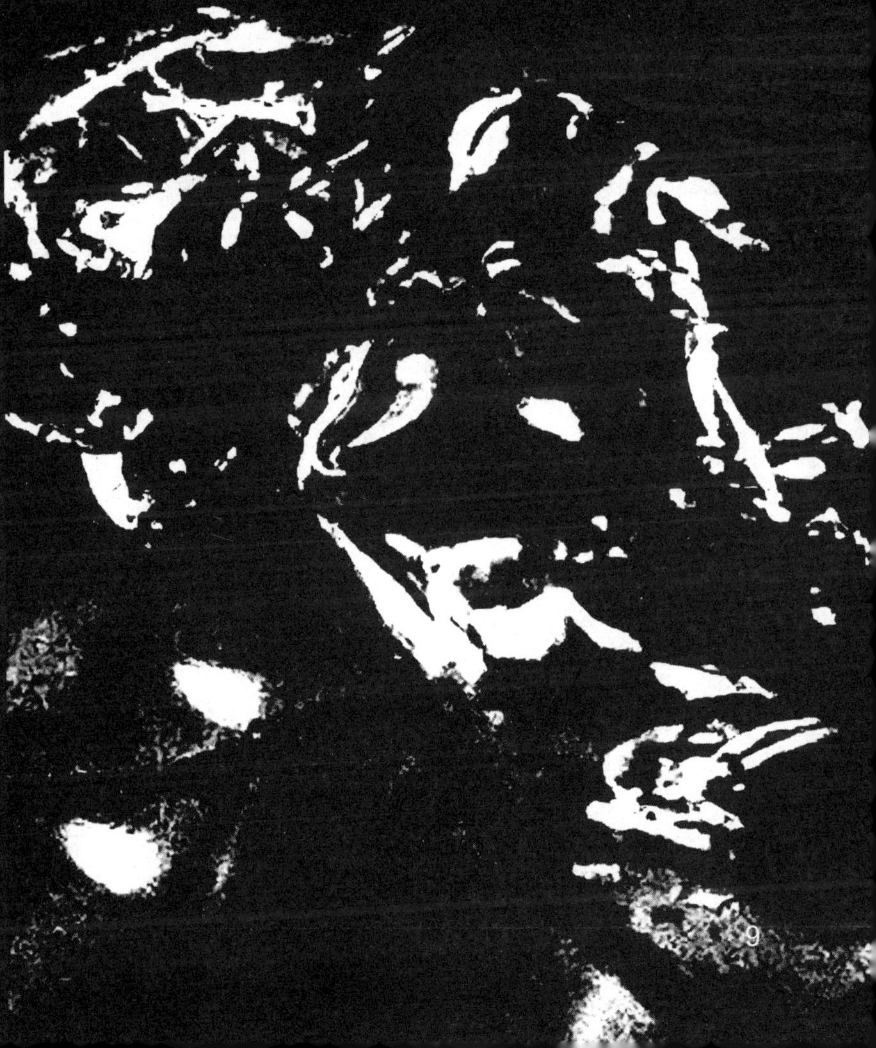

fruit divisions

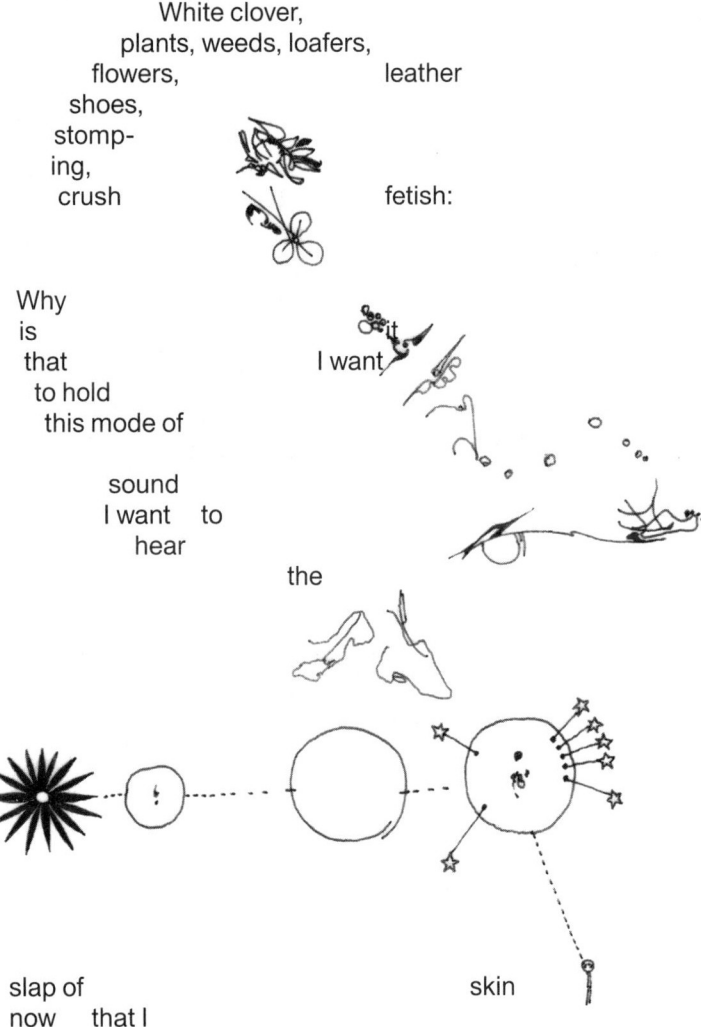

                White clover,
           plants, weeds, loafers,
        flowers,   leather
        shoes,
        stomp-
        ing,
        crush   fetish:

Why
is
 that   I want
  to hold
   this mode of

     sound
    I want   to
     hear
           the

slap of   skin
now   that I

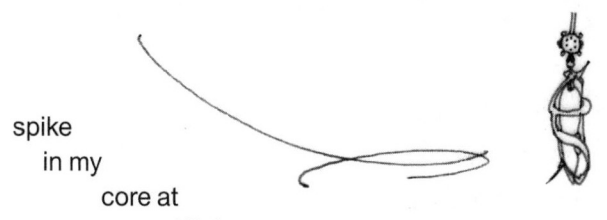

```
spike
   in my
      core at
         45 degrees
   Crouched in the grass,      I put my finger to my mouth,
                               squeeze the stem to violet nectar




         succulent silver stem
            drop lip
my fire
buzzes  my tooth responds
arching pressure

            I want to go inside
            I want to thrash
   Held in the thighs held in place
            music starts to
         fall out of me
                           it coaches fever


            qualia

   gossamer penetration


                  fruit's divisions
                           ghost package

            clean, sharp purple
```

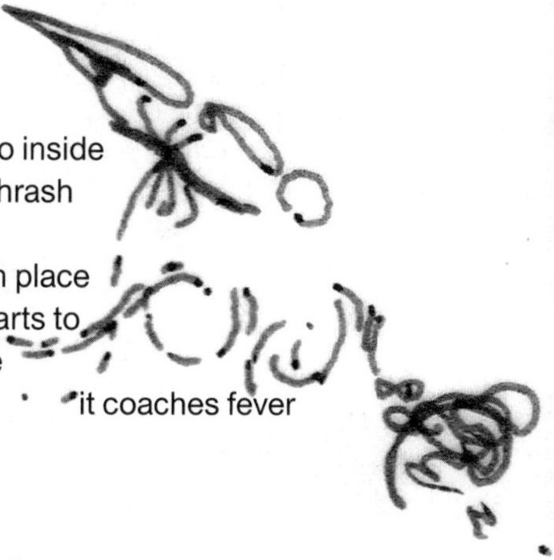

Three spells:

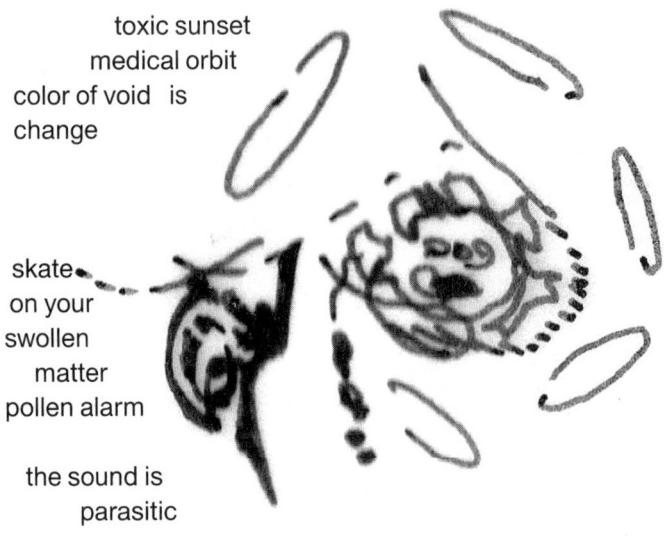

       toxic sunset
      medical orbit
color of void   is
change

skate
on your
swollen
  matter
pollen alarm

  the sound is
    parasitic

            through a danger balloon

panic zooms out

        Use wire as reins
        dominate your own sucker
        light pockets hatch all over your skin

gurgle light up and rupture
red and alarm and
rust that spits blood
swallows gray

fruit divisions

Hold onto this mode of sound and
package me as a ghost

crouched in the grass, I

                                    arch into the
                            succulent silver stem
receive the spike in my core
                spark skin
                              ache the nectar

Pressure me with fire   Catch the tip of my tongue

        White clover, weeds, plants, leather,
        flowers, loafers, stomp, crush me

nothing but an urge to puncture

adorned by scattered lace wounds

~~clean wish~~

what is love without moisture

to be Of you

made cloth
  fresh by the   end of your toes
  squeezed   one by one out of my
  mouth
  domino   clink back into form pull you
  up   to the
  ground

I   wish to
be a Tall Boy
in a lavender suit   and cherry hair
One arm out   always to reach or
greet or grab by   face by the hair and
smear me
starting   with the bubbling
lips spit   sweat friction
from   white and
                             purple

    Melter moment   when clocks fall
     cliff jump w both arms pinned to the side

Conjoining subtle and gaze your lack of intent
my frozen tongue the ribbon of violin
hands just coming short of the mouth

to forget the warning gasp

For all the flow in our love talks
there's a charred channel
of libido caught in the spider's web

I wrapped you in

plucked up
one inch at a time from the body
Giving you

   a cocoon of white noise
Breathy pawn game

hard open eyes
 a bright blue backdrop
  and the only pavement patch found on the lush
   Farm

        My hand clutching your tongue
      you my throat your eyes

              leaf hardens at touch

                place time, pull lace to me

          fingers pool around the edge of my neck
         Then
         curl into my ass
        spelling the spider

I'm
Rung by better pleasure
How to come without a capital Lover

Summer widens, letting water run, explain why until the reason finds drool

off-kilter memory a grin or a bitten face

Trying to offer you sun
Instead watch you drown in it

tangled in sheets everything blue in solitude
Brash, bicurious
confused about the face you're holding

unable to lift hands

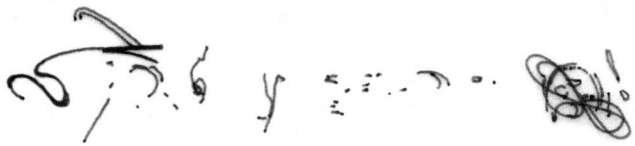

I cannot pardon your depth

explosives because love

games because conversion

remedies because beginning

what is love without moisture

I made myself Of you

I sat beneath you
letting each toe fall out of my mouth
as a crumbling keyboard

as you clink back into place what moment revives you,
I want to catch it before

I wish to be a tall boy
Kurta draped under my T-shirt, bouncy hair
with my own device for time, coiling along the metal
columns of my veins

Smear the reflection, puddles only!

Clocks fall
I leap out the window whenever

        subtle gaze stops the gasp in its tracks

but even given our chemistry

you release, squirm like a fish

your thighs your gills open
breath heat upon contact

peeling you scale by scale back until in my fingers you
are water

eyes open to a hard blue

one piece of purple left from the spring

leaf hardens at my touch
put it here, pull lakes from we

spell my neck faster
cry my ass further

okay but
it's not nothing

Lead pleasure past focus

No capital love

keep the summer near and drooling

break face

at your feet once more I offer you sun

Unable to dismiss your magnitude

rage and sweetness
manipulate and welcome
heal and reunite

what is love without moisture

I catch the moment before it revives you

sit beneath you

Chase the gasp

Of you

I leap out the window whenever

My own device for time coiling as metal in my veins

Piano corpse

toying with damp code   we
couldn't (like, *Oh, I couldn't!*)

                         begin to cradle the
                         forms of fungal
                         networks
we couldn't take   the truth of webs

Here is the hole for our face-by-face whispers
sentences finished through the ears and
gathered by this grin

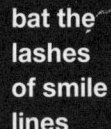

                           bat the
                           lashes
                           of smile
                           lines

        Swat perverse with a petal.
    neofurling and
                 ready
     bare—all whimper, whole figure slicked
make lace of you among the ladder

if only to spell the hover of a knife in the air

In fear before still water

let's work through
unfurl w me
hairs stand up on the arms and then *wrigglewriggle* when
the breath is back

bud—friend also flowers

skeleton we picked it up and waved its digits
astonishingly flexible and tactically
ike in it
all

at the meeting with plastic and fish bones

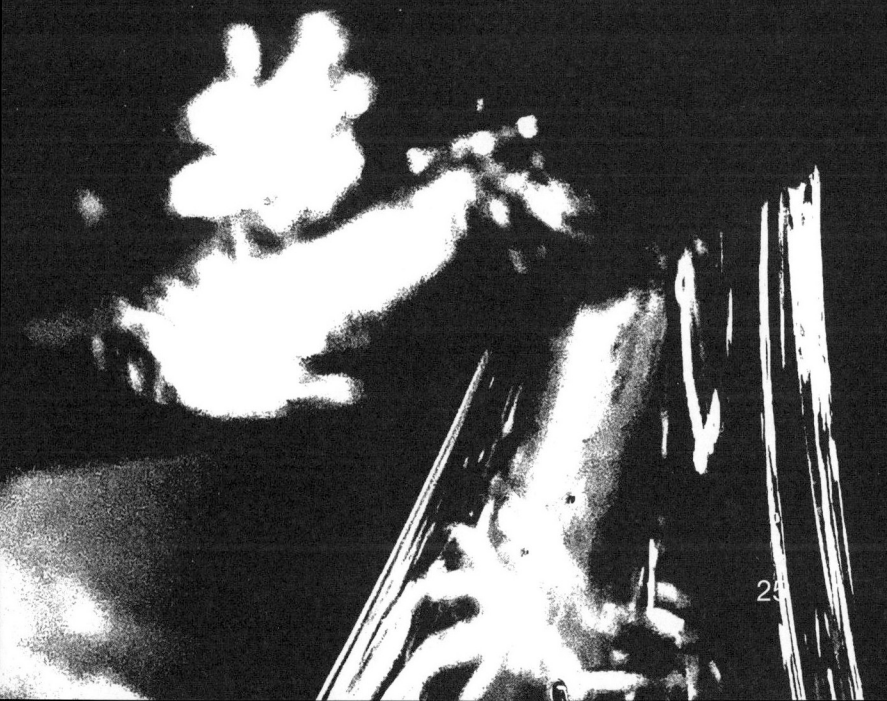

Piano corpse

Shouldn't bear it in human   hands.
      A loosened myth

   Truth, woven pulse
every   muscle of the roots

perverse petal,   neofurling, present
      bare it all with your whole body whimper

        your   beads of   sweat
     settle as lace,

       perch upon you in
         flower

Piano corpse

playing with a loosened myth
                                            we wouldn't dare to
              even try
try to decipher the system of roots
to define its weaving pulse
                            is an understanding beyond

              can't bear it in human hands
              should not

in breeze I catch a different expression than you sent me
our mood shapes distance as its own path

                            every muscle in the face
creases in delight / is it a feeling the face can't yet fathom
respond to

              tease it with a fly
                      neopose, swollen in expect
          whole figure mewing its need

make lace of you upon the climb

draw the site between the knife and the skin
desire
rustles a certain surface

come on
lift our petals
little hairs on the arms breathe back

something in my shape and function
curves into its plastic

Umbrella term

She came by to tell you about mercury

                 and a finger caught in spools of exuviae

                 It rushed in repetition

Incantations by gray
Corrosive whisper

Sun drop.   Body warmer than the towel

Hesitate, evenly, it   clasps the surface like contaminated candy floss

lipped off by small   piece

         the Body plan of an anthropod in segments

They get nervous and afraid of ladders
               confusing the rungs with their own joints

Swivel to see if anyone's watching before

hoisting their pod one   shift at a time,

           Purposeful

Spoolsofexuviae exi guide poools
exuding softer flex in dia spora
ex spear pool lip die spore awl

expand (and do wrong) the pooja

Days of suffixes, tails adjust how the
old spins, pour purpose
above pauses

A nod to their arrow

Umbrella term

Incantation of the storm
Corrosive whisper

right and wrong are made gauze and splinter

        light spools of exuviae

            rushed in repetition

Sun drop.   Body as the towel

cutting out pictures of birds
....

                                                  and flies from a book and
        they   begin to flap

the past calls to ask about a mountain and I'm
picturing five animals and the bottle
contents

you my mom grew a long, long
braid it got longer as I zoomed out and
was so far away from you   I ran to you   with
background colors changing fast and smooth climbed up
your braid   walking up so I could be on top of your head

beyond every abuse I stan my mom

remind the art white
that we've been fed irresponsibly
and trip over the medieval
gestures of blood

woof leaf fall obvious shell under shame deep fried giggles
oil splatter points thru my heart 2 a thousand plateaus

    close to the skin cut virgo nails . . . pure
    maybe a bad read

my three moods after kiss, death, bread

cutting out pictures of birds and lands

from a globe it starts to shudder

the future texts to tell me about a mountain

and I form myself an image, interlude, all goes dark,
an elephant's foot comes down onto my face, pills out

you my mother grew a long, long braid it got longer as
I zoomed out I was so far away from you I am always
so far away from you your braid at my feet I scrambled
along it the bridge the weather shifting six times and
I gathered myself at your eye level, suddenly naked in
that you could see the whole of me all at once but also
suddenly naked I'm hopeful for your heart to coax your
eyes but you take me to be an itch protect yourself
from protecting me, thunder ignored, one thunder,
tossed back to braid's end

reminded we've been fed irresponsibly
trip over blood

a howl, leaves fall, shame finds a shell
sets heart in disarranged plateaus

my three moods   kiss, death, bread

in damp posture

I am perched at a bus stop
where 5111-23 will not respond, nonchalant
and I take time to sip the air of pause
& calculate my own game
of monotony

finding stark faith amongst the Youth
at play
pushing paint
never receiving

Our new friend asks if I am a power-sub

I yell "NO"

sand coats the motion of my most tender channel
          of adrenaline
must romance only jolt into the frame in bursts?
only stand under golden light?

The right edge of your cheek
saturated peach cocktail
suddenly vibrant & hard inside styrofoam
deeply dappled contrast
a cup dependent on crumbles, dependent on the hug of dots?

I suppose we depend heavily on gas
for motion for rest for luv for laughter

in actuality, nothing solid has ever supported me

To weigh heavily on something
is to decide its shape

seal soup in pyrex & silicone
decides its only purpose is to be re-portioned, re-heated,

to get dizzy and bland

I like to imagine
how expansive and free-limbed
my soup could be

if poured upon the floor of a yoga studio,

crimson, fatty droplets, pinching into each other,

bay leaves, charred chilies, butter beans, beets,
peppercorns, ground beef

rolling freely, playing
as if I created my own tasty aquatic society

salt-water, full-bodied,

eventually seeping into the edges of the mirrored walls,
astonishingly infinite

The ultimate stretch

liquid, the kundalini champion!

I recently read a wise thing that: desire always
    exceeds any container

or, I just can never find the matching lids

One gruesome, hopeful part of me believes in the
    validity of hypocrisy
today, my coworker described the life of
    a white man as a "genre"
I wonder, what nonfiction looks like, through
    light-colored contacts?

Behavior, listed as a medical issue on the children's
health form, as something
contagious

At times, I feel proud to experience bouts of mania,
like, anything is possible!

music becomes perplexingly close,
my sideburns furrow, flows in my wrist
then, ripped from the minute,
my surroundings weep

pale orange evening:

(bracketing your cheeks
with my wet eyes)

pillow, pillar,
plucking my velour string of longing
bent grapes, sleeping grapes, resting plums, snoring blueberries

sleeping blueberries, resting grapes, snoring plums,
sleeping bumbleberries

A lance in my side, bleeding. A number for a mouth, never doubling over. What would I want wings for . . . At this point of sight (valley), there is a nervous wind tower, unmoving, purpose-planted in clay.

A long gust reflects the fish stream, shifting only thinner.

Looking at it through a clear, engraved clock face, no hands, with pale breaths, chronology begins to loosen up.

Fissure. A wall, formerly toned matte gray, is coated in high-gloss resin, its core erased by unfolding. Some inert room takes print of what it faces. Frills ironed on the cotton setting, pressed out.

Standing on the exact same spot at the exact same time— like this:

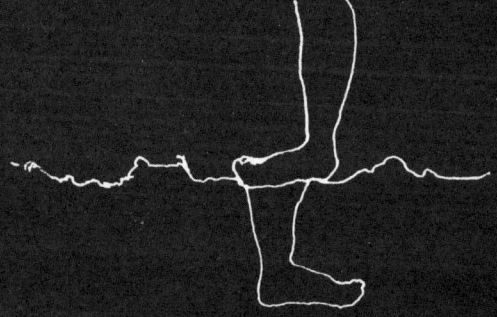

Radar intentions. Which pulse tightens around the waist? Fraction

Among everyone on the dance floor, someone dripped the ends of their Ffull-Bbodied Mmovement into the crook of my neck. Spinning yells, field on steep angle, sharp plastic, drawing blood on lips, the flaming rock, my echo of your gushing love words to me,

in this thick weather, all droplets are rendered the same, my disbelief protected by the flattening. Feet without shoes, soaking, the floor's ice of summer. All matter in seconds, pine needles sprout from my fingertips, a thin gauze grows over low limbs,

Vision in semi-colors. Fear, syncopated. Maybe when you fell out of it,

Fissure. Recalibrated chatter, failed airplane, hemorrhage, sweat in the eyes,

Then kink and self-hatred were image.

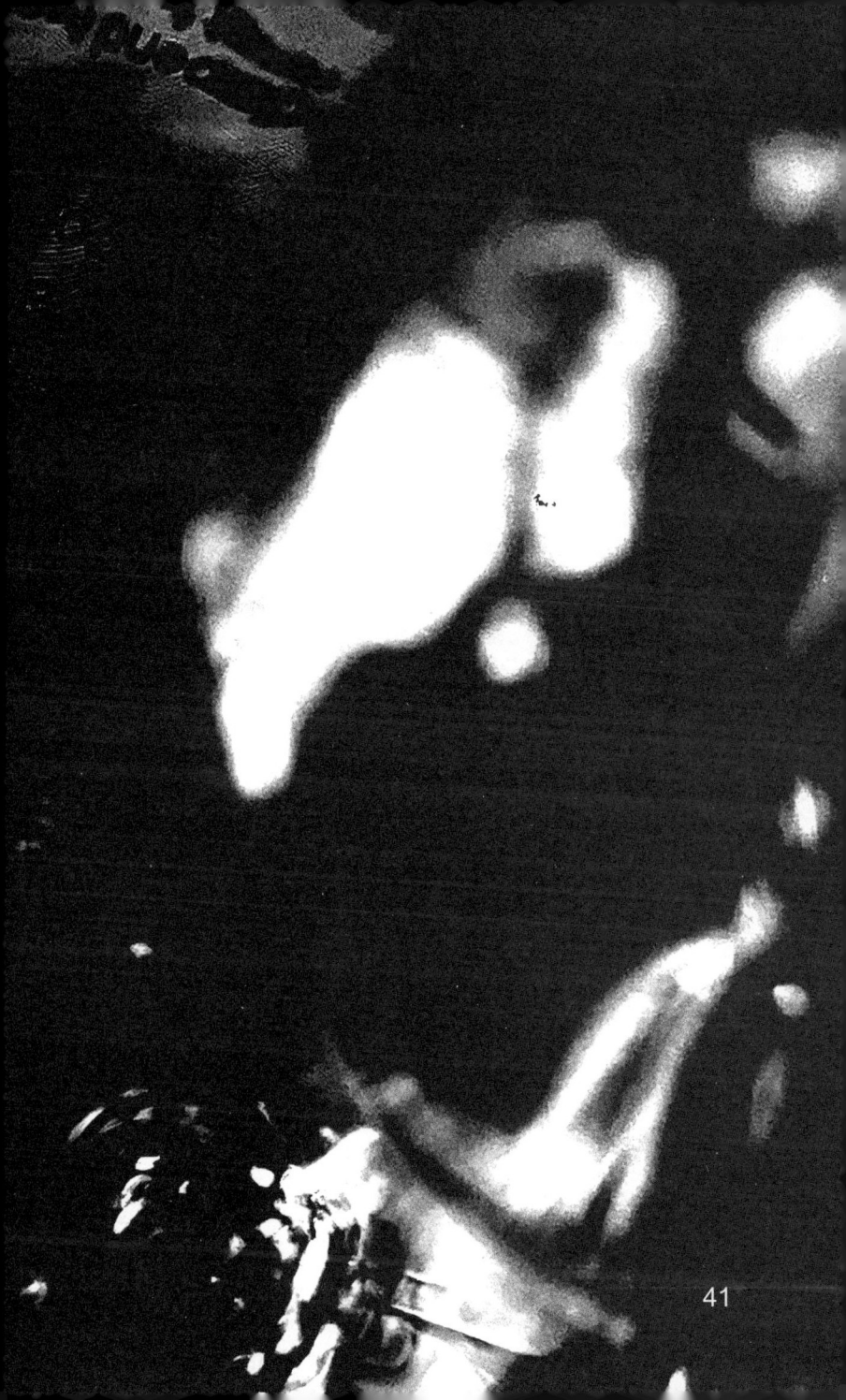

frame too early

No

she smells different every day

or rather, smells better as I know her longer

who looks up at me
        under the lashes
        thick

        weighing past
        the fuel of a dance

        a shirt inside out
            as gesture

I never knew anything   this could break my heart

        small frame
        Whimper
        bound under a hike

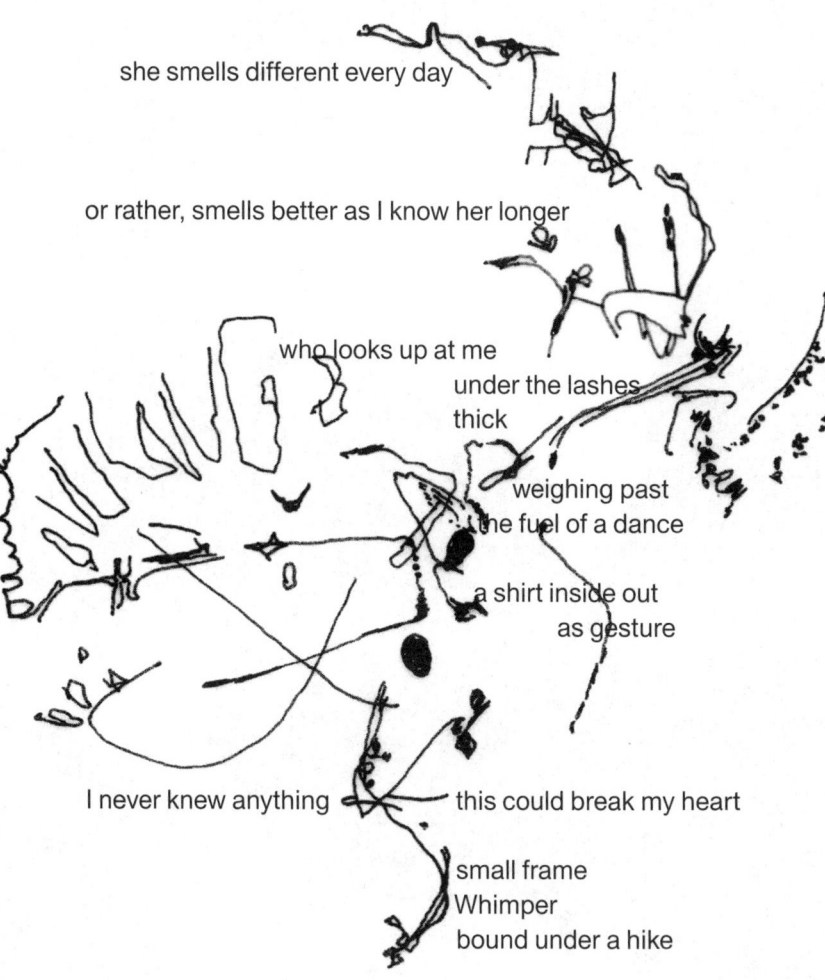

I'm
Stunted
I'm
Friday

I'm finding it easy to see you cry

Lulls, lulls,

It is a way off of road

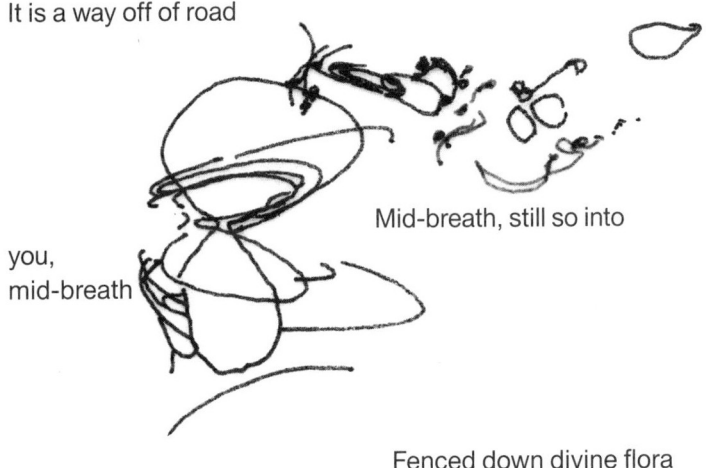

Mid-breath, still so into
you,
mid-breath

Fenced down divine flora

A true cackle, I dream of   Pine green

Ever been so happy to see

I dove into abundance of pitch

some tapped courtship
basic vindication
begin to produce melodic scheduling
and an illogical diet/cuisine
    both our tails have been gripping the same strand
                of sea grass
                for several days

                changing colors

my waiting knuckles
have started to bleed

pressed against the back of my teeth
allowing only curled murmurs to leak
losing oxygen

fresh notion
if we had a dog we would still be together
some need to watch the other love someone
that they don't want to fuck

falling is in the whistle

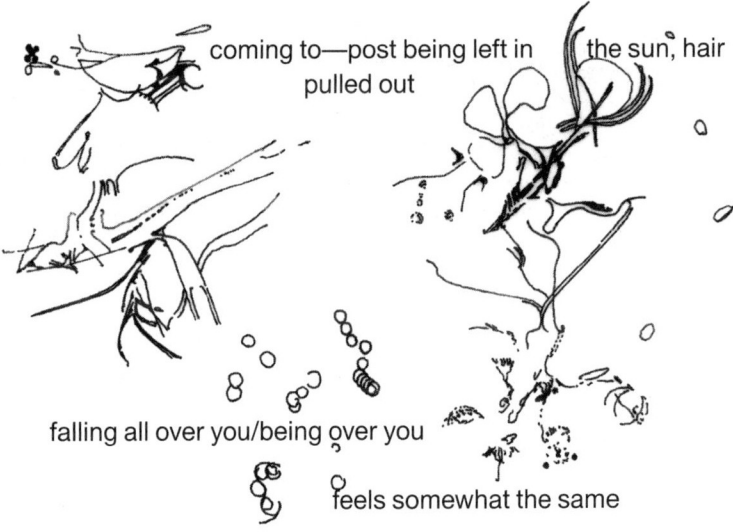

coming to—post being left in the sun, hair pulled out

falling all over you/being over you

feels somewhat the same

frame too early

Yes

she smells different every day

actually, smells

                                                            better

as I know

                                            her

longer

look up at me
thick under the lashes

the diagonal fuels a dance

                moments where it springs out, joints loosen
as waves, unlock an overwhelming gust
currents from neck to fingernail

come undone for you

                I didn't know this
                it could break easily

its body a whimper
                bound by a climb

     I'm
     Spring
     I'm
     Monday

I'm finding hurt simple

   comma, glide

      off-road

    comma

please turn away

release the flora

Found demon within a laugh, dreamt a color I didn't know

Ever been so happy to see

I dove into abundance of pitch

changing colors
over several days
the strand of sea grass
both our tails grip
begin to produce
an illogical diet and
melodic scheduling
spark this
reprieve
spark
surrender

Tie ribbons to cut my heart from my head
knuckles bleed, losing oxygen

falling is in the whistle
coming to—having been left in the sun, hair pulled out

falling all over you/being over you feels somewhat the same

low flame

My yesterdark in 8 pm

is a charm today

tremor start to look like sparkle

made way with the sudden
      balm of blue

fingered the hem of
      a turtleneck
           laying on the table corner

headlight I manipulate image I roll my eyes in search of you
squeeze the shirt collar collar into its own narrow

breath crosses through a straw pull the

most tear-like leaves from the path

waxy curves eye light

danced by crayon

faster walk   my blinks harp

a comb of silk threads are
dominoed

run along the octave

carving nails along each leaf's vein
in anime where girls run home from school
in the rain with books held above their heads

Me   Watching lightning storms   Back to the window

eaten like a drawer open and shut

the comic of its bones stripped clean

Just the corner of a painting seen through a mirror

a ribbon tied around a bomb

When every day is not perfect with
you I do not worry

Bells
Triple sadness

flexible pulse

Ways of looking . . .   painting is all about
love but honestly only if the gays do it ;)

empty scratches   everyone peeks past the grip
     or risk

turn to the lip of eye travel,

inexplicable weeping

spread over the curve of the round table

flipping through a wet ratio   there cannot be
color knowledge

This is how much I miss you talking
Swift flap. Eager and hungry, dripping with forward focus,
you stitched yourself along the bridge
to reach, to stand not upon but above, the peak
and its shimmer,
wild wonderer, risking a lullaby,
and stay there, hiding just to peer into the waters, the
original ultramarine
where spectral, sponge-tinged turtles
were rising from the blue

There the taut static of nature at its lowest,
humming, veering frequencies,
baseless declarations!

A great gasp of your forearms,
a laugh, at you, but nice
absorbing the liminal, moving the pause.

Steps forward—a train—sleeping so fast.
A puzzling finesse,

How could you help falling out of yourself on such a lust for
the color of glass—
you, involuntary normals, imagined concrete,
a burning light, wax refuses to budge
in the face of the overeager, the endearing greed
of wanting the moon in the day and the sun in the night!

low flame

My yesterdark of 8 pm

comes to me today as lure

tremor start to look like sparkle

          spin spells from
      the blue open

            I roll my eyes in search of you

        find you making surface porous

When everyday is not perfect with you I do not worry

                      Bells
                      Triple sadness

walk fast   blinks harp
                  silk threads domino

run along the octave

watching lightning storms   my back to the window

a fish eaten like a drawer open and shut
the comic of its bones stripped clean

a ribbon tied around a bomb
flexible pulse
flipping through a wet ratio   there cannot be
color knowledge

This is how much I miss you talking

Flutter. Esurient, ready, sweating toward it,
you belted yourself with a bridge
to grasp, to be not at but of
the core and its glimmer
boundless imaginary, harmonic priority
then pause there, veering just barely to glimpse
the moonspun river, the truth of silver
where iridescent, barnacled turtles
were rising from the blue

There the stretched dust of cosmos at its ground
Purring, arching measure,
erratic exclamations!

Your wingspan's deep inhale,
our secret banter
soak up the threshold,   kindle the still

walk closer—chariot, slowness in crash
delicate trick,
How could you stop tumbling
past yourself under thirst for a mirrored answer?
you, compulsive usuals, chimeral bond
low flame, overcome motion
against leaky yearn, charming lust
of wanting the moon in the day and the sun in the night!

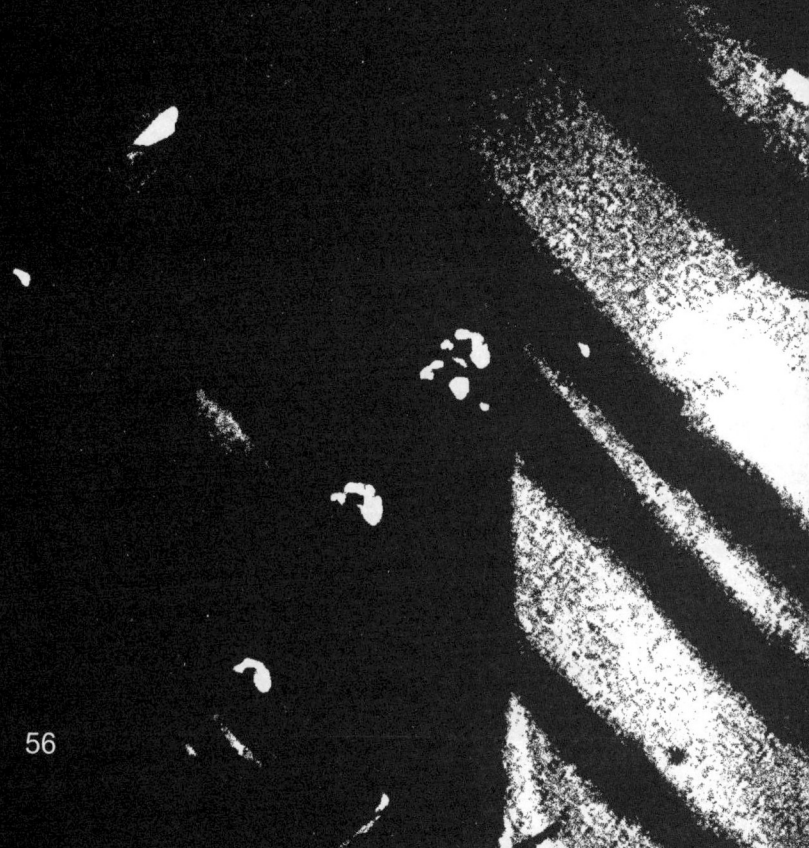

low flame

My
 in 8 pm

is a charm today

        tremor starts to look like sparkle

      made way with the sudden
          balm of blue

     fingered the hem of
       a turtleneck
                       laying on the table corner

I manipulate image   I roll my eyes in search of you
      squeeze the shirt collar collar
into its own narrow

breath crosses
through a
                    straw pull the

most tear-like   leaves from the path
          waxy curves eye light

              danced by crayon

    faster walk   my blinks harp

                a comb of   silk threads are
                          dominoed

                 run along the octave

          carving nails along each leaf's vein

like an anime where girls run home from school in the rain with books held above their heads

I watch lightning storms   Back to the window

eaten like a drawer open and shut

the comic of its bones stripped clean

Just the corner of a painting seen through a mirror

a ribbon tied around a bomb

                                    When every day is not perfect

with you I do not worry

Bells
                              Triple sadness

               flexible pulse

Ways of looking . . .   painting is all about love
honestly only if the gays do it

empty scratches   everyone peeks past the grip
      or risk

turn to the lip of eye travel,

inexplicable weeping

          spread over the curve of the round table

flipping through a wet ratio   there cannot be color knowledge

This is how much I miss you talking

Swift flap. Eager and hungry, dripping with forward focus,
you stitched yourself along the bridge
to reach, to stand not upon but above, the peak and its shimmer,
wild wonderer, risking a lullaby,
and stay there, hiding just to peer into the waters, the original ultramarine
where spectral, sponge-tinged turtles
were rising from the blue

There the taut static of nature at its lowest,
humming, veering frequencies,
baseless declarations!

A great gasp of your forearms,
a laugh, at you, but nice
absorbing the liminal,   moving the pause.

Steps forward—a train—sleeping so fast.
A puzzling finesse,

How could you help falling out of yourself on such a lust for the color of glass—
you, involuntary normals, imagined concrete,
a burning light, wax refuses to budge
in the face of the overeager, the endearing greed
of wanting the moon in the day and the sun in the night!

imaginary design

downloading   Latest relapse

    dipped into everything else

    thing of darkness
a spur tail you found
just walking through the desert
twelve feet long and
    squirm and flailing

the dot and the line
hi what are you reading now?
thoughts that might be useful in the future

      the bird in love with honey
    has fallen in
multiheaded or
multiple in some other way

exhales fire and smoke

        ate this and burst it open

        open

nowhere region

slow hand on mischief

        three heads turn this
          way at once

my ears need to stick out of   my hair

    if it takes a rock   takes glue
                      I squeeze your pulling inner

imaginary design

fear it'll relapse
or

everything else will seep in

the path we had then, darkening now

a dismembered tail you found
on both sides of the road
twelve feet long
held and trembling

middle, eclipse distance
what are you most present for?
something to describe the past

your familiar absorbs every age
breathes fire onto a scaffold

open
nowhere region

if it takes a frame
takes ice
I squeeze your pulling in

5:56

Putting on your filmy dress
I'm immediately surrounded by
the oily fragrance of you

my ambivalence is annoying
you say in bed, curving narrow fingers into a C under my chin
pad fingertips
against the top inch of my throat
just short of my want
I falter
at what loosens, shifts,
in the open wax of a morning
6:20 am can't be anything but essayist

erratic fault of someone claiming their original "aura"
a short necklace secret account
and a dubious data pool

she has this extended handle on the vision of my body

on the frame of femme
my groans curl in verse

with a dead gaze, breath gets spent here

this morning repeats
each time I am like, um, yeah, after you describe your thing
and roll my eyes counterclockwise
each time hair wraps around my finger

three blades of raw libido sometimes while dancing fell out
of my hands

in the slip of a moment
etched and patterned with
casual, casual love

late sleep rearranges gets our shadows wrong

the changing globe light
hovers on blue
stroking in place with the memory

My aeon cuts the body
inherent pleasure gnaws on the hip

swear I am not in reach

I practice the word Sprung
but really, my ankle curls around the probability
of someone wanting or could or maybe wanting
maybe or would could   wanting to orbit

5:56

the oily fragrance of you
I'm surrounded
ambivalent
I falter

In bed you cup my chin
won't let me have it
won't press harder

what loosens in dawn's divide
can't describe this time without something
wistful
doubt the supposed aura

on the frame of femme
my groans curl inverse

hollow gaze, breath spent

this morning repeats
counterclockwise

immersed in dimension
three blades slip a moment
etch and pattern it with your orbit

in verse

speaking is left out of my mouth as it's unable to play still
in
each verse has a new pattern
there are lakes of residue under my palms
writing my verse it's all lowercase and
there are no spaces between the words
it's a pouring mesh that
hovers in the web between toes and pierces through as your
wrist glides over that
perfect dimple prying my ass
verse 1, verse 2 seems faster
could be anything for you
could do it and look the
opposite way

far from old posing
switching in order to
take the exact part of what they

want
a sex in verse.

with this part

that changes
there under the harder light
in verse or
then verso

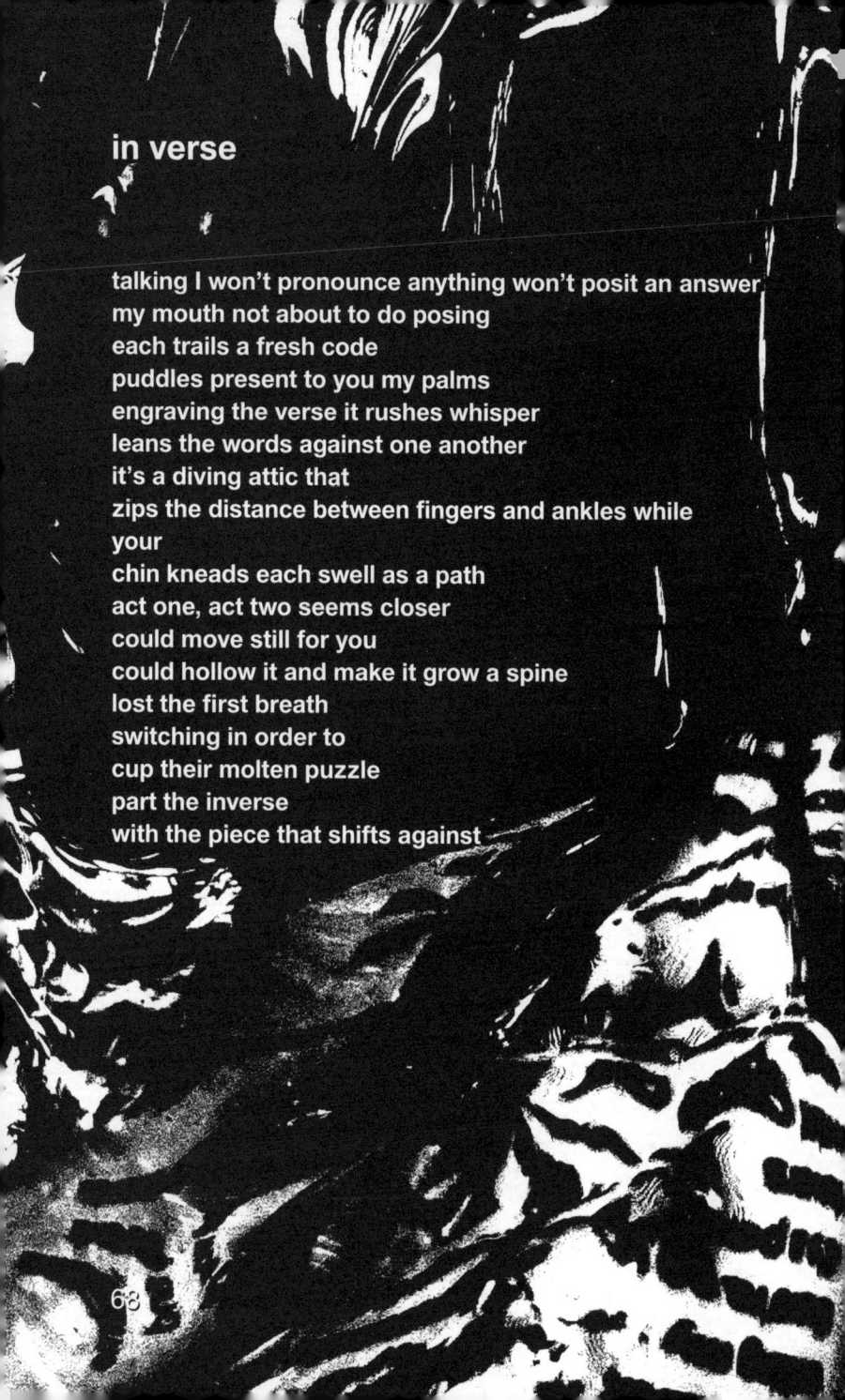

in verse

talking I won't pronounce anything won't posit an answer
my mouth not about to do posing
each trails a fresh code
puddles present to you my palms
engraving the verse it rushes whisper
leans the words against one another
it's a diving attic that
zips the distance between fingers and ankles while your
chin kneads each swell as a path
act one, act two seems closer
could move still for you
could hollow it and make it grow a spine
lost the first breath
switching in order to
cup their molten puzzle
part the inverse
with the piece that shifts against

Purr

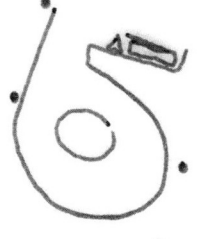

I would like a giant bird to just chill on my chest
bitch everything you do turns to pearl
If memory could bloom
Fold down the flurry and catch its corners
in the smile you can't prevent
I'm happy, happy with your sheepish purr
pull hard again on my morning
one more dash of
miracle chain
wander rush

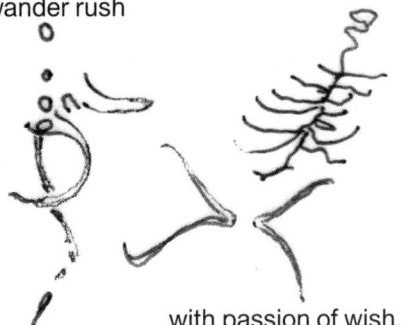
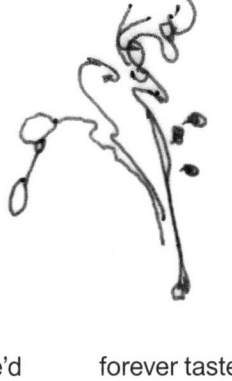

        with passion of wish, we'd   forever taste
  red
sun that makes me want to crawl under covers

    embodiment not a place to reach
    it only felt bad when I was with you
croon bug
softer pad

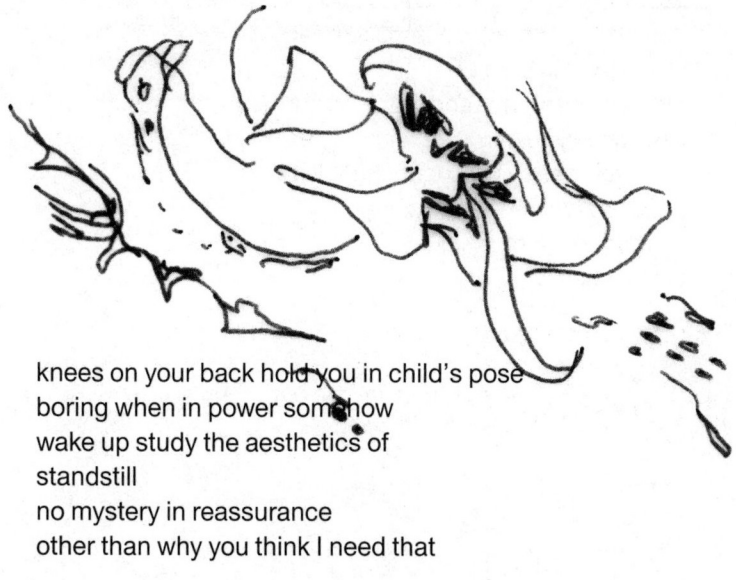

knees on your back hold you in child's pose
boring when in power somehow
wake up study the aesthetics of
standstill
no mystery in reassurance
other than why you think I need that

the kind of brown who prefers urgent care over
self-care but uninsured I guess what I can seek out is
organic cleaners massage cosmetic drugs and a
tank top that heats the swell with or without compression

Purr

How can you suggest I'm chilling
when this pattern starts to grow from me
bitch if only we had wands for hands
Sip on your answer let it live long
Tighten roots of need, free wheels of need, pull once more
on the dusk chain
one more sparkle
one more forgiven
my leash is endless water
         escaping flame

the beige sky   my worst fear

If one could find loose binding, uncovered book stitch

In the corner puddle of the well-known lobby . . . reflecting

The beige sky

My worst fear

Even though I tell white people

I am afraid of nothing

Nothing but

My brother getting hurt

Or, as small as possible, unable to see one another

& losing my memory

Lol what

But about just before me, you

Step left, brush "dirt away" on

The sidewalk, as if your toe is

Delicate, as if you think about it

All the time, little bits of dirt,

Never listening . . .

Should I question my smile face

Aftermath theories

Slow, indie breakfast

A finger wrapped around mine, not tight, but

Curly, firm as a well-pigmented colored pencil

Well?

well, my safe word is

always ravioli

It's

Supercalefragilisticespialadocious

It ranges lol

Butttttt always lands between

Four to five syllables

The life of a libra

"I can't seldom relate"

Arm in arm

This part of my finger is

hooked together on either side

Stuffed into my most ambiguous pocket

these, the one before, I just said,

and the one after, I'm going to say,

don't even feel like they have come

Out of me

Formed

through general design optics

A color-all game, a swirling

tangent, all of a sudden, have

babbled on about fire escape

horror and Sade and the safety of an avenue

When you are gone from its

beginning, trying to deliver a map

of clarity (wandering off, clipped

the end of a two-tailed story)

Your worst quality, you try to codify

"clear," make it superficially poetic,

Ply and mould through.

Always wondering what happened

before bed

when my eyes were wide open, but

dried out!   And wrestling with

sinews of skipping currents

Slow panic, thinking about what all

the sleeping adults were resting

about before the revolutionary movie

november three ago

Talks and talks and talks, spins, take your medicine,
my hair curlers spin thoughts, everything is flat
dead neutral, gray that lacks purple, only curves
industrially, a factory, so many living parts, so much
fucking money . . .

Would be cool to return to that raw giggling phase
Like putting pillows all over your senses to go to
the moon, the same as making out just to make out
nobody's trying to make you it's just tongue play

and that's just it, shut up about that nostalgia, these
things weren't stolen, you are lost now at this moment
at 6:23 pm. Ever so blue within technology, limited fog,
covered in scanner codes.

Would be cool to get back to that raw state
of not needing to describe immediately after

Inconsequential and therefore in touch with later
moments in life, thoughts on the spiritual, on objects
of assumption, on displacement.

Culturally appropriating from my own grandmother, sick thoughts, pretending I don't know how to put some throat in pronouncing my last name. Thoughts in the raw feeling, lying in a sensory deprivation pool, $50 an hour? Costs so much to lose yourself pleasantly. Me, a child still, trying to restore some sort of blurry eyesight, wear no glasses at the computer. Trying to match the queer thoughts. Letting blocks blur, lines overlap. Restored, stronger than the loss as it is remembered . . . A new separate life of its own.
The politics of a hypothetically official color. Holographic, seriously reflective, absorbent too. Brings people back to life they say, the great ones. With a big G.
Mashallah.
Unquestioning. Thankful for trembling, thankful for the purr and grunt of an automobile, thankful we don't always produce throttling death, although we usually do.

Must we then pick up the pieces? How to do this, if things fall into each other. Intertwined puzzle, the most significant. Blinded by Windows. Those who don't experience fear won't let me have it . . .
The old modes, creeping up through the floor. I don't want you to touch me, even if you're my neighbor, don't want you to touch me, even if you are family, don't want you to touch me, even if you understand Urdu. Sticky winter, I will only teach your children, I will never lose my hard gaze, me, restless and full of libido that will never involve you.
Somewhere in a flatland, dust creeps in when we push our beliefs . . . death crows, rolls into reddened earth, vslaps everyone in the face, thank goodness we can turn somehow.

Nobody asked me to stay here and I don't have to.
There isn't space enough

But I want to be mildly original, to change my name, for fun, not fear, but still fear, trying to make it fun. I asked my parents if I could be Mowgli, a shirtless little boy, if I could be named Bungalow, something airy, balanced, one level, lacking hierarchy.

The stage set of history . . . not enough dimension for you to step up.
Soooo lovely, the lists of things the men have done, compiled into great paintings, hours of paint, hours of blood, hours of silence, hours of complacency, hours of handheld beauty, hours of rape,
And then, we faint, sigh back
Finally able to see only dark, yelling, panting in cold air so to see my anxiety out loud. You're radical ladies, wouldn't you have slept well this week, you blend into comfort, you're protected, you match the walls. You love love but you steal everything else you don't love brown people you love the earth, you look to see yourself in a suit.

I'm here, confused on Fridays, foul on Sundays. let me love airplanes. Let me fear as you fear a little glimpse of Arabic, sounds harsh you say, kind of hard on the tongue.

March on for her, don't speak to me, don't speak to my brother, don't ask me about my childhood, don't share me, I don't want me in your paragraph. Twerk it white girl. You can do anything.

drama guarantees it

Today's fiction is dish soap
rain, the safe cruise

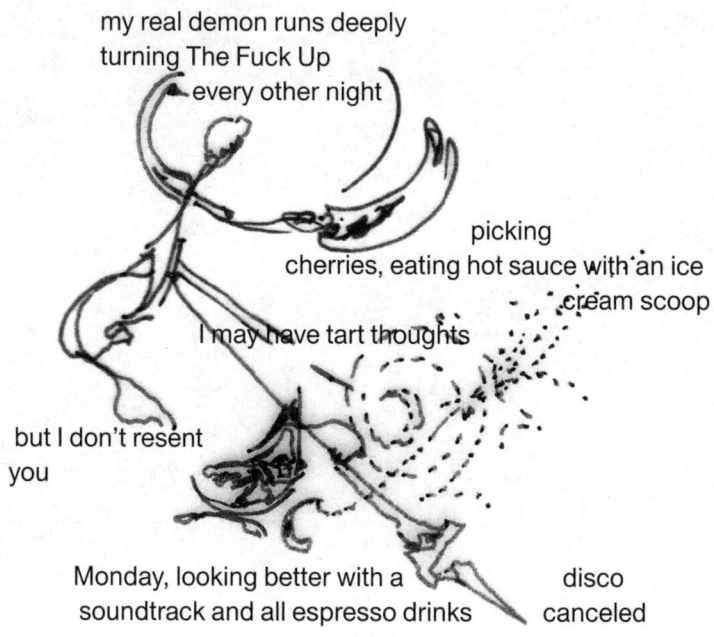

      my real demon runs deeply
      turning The Fuck Up
          every other night

                      picking
        cherries, eating hot sauce with an ice
                            cream scoop
    I may have tart thoughts

but I don't resent
you

    Monday, looking better with a   disco
      soundtrack and all espresso drinks   canceled

I assumed it wasn't meant like that
flowery retelling of my day only tolerable in song
finally ready to be difficult
measuring waves
                    I am thriving

drama guarantees it

Your poetry a prank of relation
my real demon curdles your grammar, picks a fight with a
nail file against each comma, nudge past articulation
Against a week shape, frost dial, condition of the cackle
This time if you address the margin as the best part
you'll find that you'll stop complaining
and let them be
thrive actually
give them everything you have I really mean that
measure every exercise you calculated as an invention and
cancel it
and point to the edge of it
there there is a gushing waterfall
finally

an exploded gate
an exponential garden
fur and claws pirouette from the roots of every leaf
so much needed life skin purrs as a swimming surface

Instamorph

Instamorph

How easily you cry laugh flirt flight   etc.

Musical syrup

What's undone

Hesitated scream

Button

mapped agreements

Nailing it all over flowers   pain in one cyclical party

my dry erase mirror
an incomplete eggshell

a collected fantasy
press delete

September comes and you've called me a pervert
six times already
It's very boring

I could be your arch support
swimming the line between fish and fist

Tiny clocks on the wrist make me, exclusively alive,
delight in ironic free play

Your miraculous grin oozes around
lack of smell looming

An arm dangling from a windowsill,

The Most Wish
   trapped inside an unopened lemon

or the   wing behind the past of our hug

thoughts   of introducing mosquitoes into our sex

tiny clocks on the wrist
delightedly wish forth

Is it possible that we   feel Nothing

Instamorph

How simple it seems that you
smile moan curse play etc.

how regular for me to
lose your breath

My scream undone
with j one button

with that my Yes was mapped

print

naughty child
thrilled by new punishment
totally innovative
they think, tongue dogging out

all that matters
what is raised enough
to make the
screenprint copy

turn the window off

twinkle
the same as lowercase i miss u
save for the added ellipses
I brush your intention back
a plastic putty
that lets me carry around a support for your smile

while u lick me
I examine my toes
and 50 percent of my face at 37 percent opacity
nodding pinky

my toenails dissolve to reveal
an ascending row of rose-hued sunchokes, braised,
shimmering

slowly twist
then pop, they open, race to bloom
far too fast

13 thick clear bugs scatter in a bending V
become a single gossamer wing
the blue taut
withheld from flight

as your mouth finds me

my eyes make
a stone on black gelatin

silk is brought painfully close
it dances by, pirouettes all showy and whatever
then, it rips
loses the stone

when I come
my printer finally starts to work
spewing out like 57 pages
canceled jobs

the document cuts off the words taking the form of tape left
on the toner roll

Shireen becomes hire resume is sum

we lay all over each other
then collect the prints
match together in a grid
        revealing the butterfly

        woof leaf fall obvious shell under shame deep fried
            giggles oil splatter points thru my heart 2
                a thousand plateaus

      close to the skin cut virgo nails . . .   pure
            maybe a bad read

my three moods

after kiss, death, bread

Did not for a moment stop blinking

twisted hands behind my head
Pretend everything is love so everything gets moisture, the drip
stands on top and refused reflect
Hi angel
you're allowed to feel everything at once
pages and pages it's okay if you can't connect
today can't speak
Today
my phone cannot sparkle that is
the mood today
Demons out
Today
your blank tongue calling to each eye

Did not for a moment stop blinking

put it back over me dress me find my shelter
eyes contact you in glue
ribbon limb pitch hard to roomed corners
Feign this as love so as to indulge precipitation
if it refuses to fall what ends the drop
Ok baby
you can do a lot of moods at once it's
ok all weather is your handful it's okay if you can't expand
today can't word
today can't
present
today
my pen is the tongue that owns me
that is the
bitch of today
allow me to release
today
freak orion today
rip the bubble from your speech

Using my own body as a hammock

$300 cyber boots
a small skipping lamb
using my own body
as a hammock to sleep in
gliding and leaping among trees
profiles anger hidden by careful angles, long lashes
choose one of these light sources as the start to your
journey out of here
plant hatches from an
egg and arms
unfold to
show mass of
spores of flies
frosted
grapes
vacant hybrids
squeaky ass gum voice
convinced it only   sounds like that on the phone
fire in the heart   of a patient tree
laced leather
choking maile
feeling   confused/
excited
about   decorated dogs
my fantasy   —>   you hold me
by a metal ribbon   seven feet long
tied to the stem of   a powder blue apple
a servile robot   with bunny ears

a servile robot with bunny ears
and one perfect cloud shaped foot
my eyesight, thankfully getting worse
so that the spider walks on the sky

in some directions my giantess draws blood
offers bridges
swallows me whole
on a good day the light on a dolphin's fin and a monkey
crawling on the ledge of a mountain palace make me lose it
start to weep
my blood tongue
so inspired by images

pulling you to my chest by your petals
watch the sun leave libra
and begin to set at five
turning my teeth out noise up paws out
walking on all fours
sound would have distracted you
it looks like water
protecting most what looks like and moves like ourselves

I want to sit in
a snake lol
retro fetishism
I don't like
nostalgia girls
I don't like what
used to happen
to us
imagine
gay ass Po
the Teletubby
walking the
digits
of Tokyo data
smiling   in the harsh wind

no world   before temperature

the heavens a mind, finale

the bound
was I caught ice on   hill
points
and then there   were
days   the moon felt

like it would cut you open

I went to the mall coated in
Thé Noir perfume
my perfume was like my date

it was the "mirror figure"
the finale it's saying

I saw again and   this time
could pick up shadows
in their face for nuance

gather the creases,   so to speak

    now

    the blue   falters, fog blades
    violet
    and
    their frank   plain talking style

    the bound   was the mirror
    figure

now the first time

                          I caught sight of ice on

hills
like tendons

now that I'm   drawing a story about
their
time
and   features in
their
time
they looked like tendons

the heavens a mind, finale

the rein was/the restraint was
my freezing point, sooner than expected
the curse having tripped my circulation

There was the day nobody could question that
the moon's form could shadow total presence
shatter the day and its surroundings
it was winking in that it knew it did that know it had redirected
the temperature of orange, the mood a malleable channel
my face fell agape looking up and froze open
mouth in lunar mirror

Seeing them in return, now I could find nuance in their
character folds

but to wonder in blue, the moon's arid gust
threw daggers in the colloidal mesmory, the cool shade aghast

the restraint was a new curse, notes uncounted, unable to
withstand a breeze, or shift, in that retreat into surface

Machynis,
..............•........

                  hold this for
Good, don't fare the balance of a
calm soil and
ideal weather, last in exalt
eluding the how of
how to know mortal
by that I mean you not me but then you were
obsessed with   and   that was

A condition where you could not see anything but your own
eyes reflected back at you right in front of you inrealtime
hollow graphic on tail it didn't quite
call or view or dim at this view

the last edit was seconds ago

There isn't a space of entrance. The timing is so close walls
of rain with no light around hug your figure. As if you are
pushed to the ground by pouring force, but you are

are still standing, though you may not want to, stuck rigidly upright what is dropping and beating like soaked bells is a weighted blanket, you are held in this place your sigh prolonged so far as it is not quite breath but is not less and your sense is not of how you got there.

The door opens quickly and without a handle no vision of what wind might have pulled it ajar. Blinding light falls, shuts off the shape of the rain you could not see before and grabs hold of you pulling right out, through the next door even though you have just begun to surrender to "it told you so."

Empty space to look around, empty space recognize what becomes of

Your figure taken
        Doors and doors after the other placed too close together, and a puddle that flows thin carpet all under the edge of them, ticking back
                      A vulnerable coda

the surge of pop

                Sing along to water

blunt imaginings

            evade collision

                    jade speed

magic map application

find my way into the tomb

Machynis,

I dare you to take me as your familiar
Don't wait for the mercurial cycle,
ideal weather

Suddenly you are five ages at once

In that

so far as it somehow landed
on the same place

you around it
and how come warm or comfort lands in between

where face yes is vulnerable and torso is
a word we spit rid it from our mouths
at the same time gasp laughing
sorry bro to me to ourself to you

and my problem here is I'm supposed to speak of joy
but I am circling my self because I've spent it
to shun you or I assume that's where I've driven us

but here's one mommy chuckle slap it on the neck
and look at me with
one drop of water that tells me
you're caught
with a quick ear

how else to insist on the angled speak
hands gift it not right in front of my face
eyes open and the search pattern has a way of coaxing
spine charge
knowing that
I'd rather follow the dance
or make new moves
in heat together

gum on the counter
formula written on the thigh

on the mirror
please do not refer to me

but want me
and sit inside that
tear your teeth in

cannot love one
another well because
it's this ice thing our spark stuff
and the melt sits itself down at some point

desire and pride here

a dance carries

it is maybe simply a carry

                condensation
                spit
                the reframing
                frames
                race
                an imagined intimidation
                another love
                where tension spins

here watching the surface spin
and a body flat

and a body flat
the hegemony

the tilt of a cocoon spectacles
another body

I want it so badly that I cannot
even write anymore can't even speak anymore
cannot explain myself to
you because whatever made the warmth
have generative spools caught the wrong edge and
mistangled and
now you've turned away

separated by
our own selfish narratives
our own pulse of it our steps in the sand but neither
saw the other do the step at the same time   where's trust when
it comes from the unknowing, can't continue

if only made by memory
moon I walk up I'm running on the beach that's
the best way I dissolved boundaries
run on the shore
to run from you, to run from it, at a time
where one is not usually awake
meant I would be yours
moons shadow
after it together
the metal puddle

melted silver and pearl

can't control exactly where it lands
lands lopside last pool
little lip of lapiz
to toy with it
is running for a light that won't come closer
the present is the only option
and our moment was a gift to me

spill baby trying it all out together ease together heat and
frustration and impress me here
could be better for you
teach you I'm thoughtful
5 am red
light and a racing bike ride only focused on the
thrill where's the back of it the bone of it no comfort in the
hands

to overrun the form and the theater,   it bites as a
mess of the flex
and
not the
gash of it

the meek transfer, snap to it, and never in break

looping to gain full control
   blue ocean plugin 1.23.3

in search of collaboration
with me
head cocked
rinse the soup smell

and did we
so coherently shall we

There is a stretch in my mind that blurs

we're not out of the storm yet but I take yours

occasionally leaving blueish marks

**so far as it somehow landed
on the same place**

and comfort is rid from our mouths
at the same time as a gasp as a laugh cannot help but spill
out at risk of needing to be sorry

circling your quick ear
to insist on an angled way of speech
I'd rather make new moves
choreography on the mirror

please do not refer to me

it's an ice thing our spark stuff
and the melt sits itself down at some point

desire and pride
spit or condensation
frames
race
imagined intimidation

the cocoon spectacles this other body

separated by selfish narratives
only see our own steps in the sand

in running for a light that won't come closer
the present is the only option

should run from you
in the moons shadow
melting silver and pearl

together there never was collaboration
leaving blueish marks

echo-graphic

At fancy the bird slants its formula
In picture the bird circles its own call
In the pine the bird lashes oddity
The screams scroll
the veins catch bass and relation

To coat the torus
As in your neck walls are magnet

made outline open   as mist
nap portioned
hand of test

                       agitate the course
                           tantric gest
                     a pithy statement

The balance

Stormed in,   flashes of dust, scabs
           and alarm tone a tail directed
             to the current. Print.

         This the figure that follows you
     I spotted your guest
this is your painter
     the guise I hoped to fumble through

Like a choreography, melting figurines, our elegant twitch
of surface

Solaris, rubied and lengthened by clearings, ponds, hills
that curve their
root arms inward

Let's chill at the surface beyond
my pliant wish, a simple frog to gild your order
at the curdles of glass—a hovering partition
sex falling, trailing ligament, the greener show
bailed by this leaking order, it knocks out

echo-graphic

at creation the crow skews its rite
in portrait surrounds its own cry
through the forest its wings trace erratics
the voices fold
canyon finds truth and alto

to quilt the halo
as in your neck walls are magnet

told path to burst afloat
rest segments
finger steps

The stasis
                spills out, rays of ash, scars
      and scare tune a stem directed
to the current. Smile.

        This the icon that dates you
            I caught your counter
     this composer
      the face I hoped to

let the bodies hit the floor
•••

I'm down for thorough because I'm down for the light's tickle
in one while might
not have the energy to hold anything
but hoped to catch the storm view before the sky turned off
really she told me we might have ghost pipe on the upper
path. where the
grief urged my mud feet where it urges surprise

the lip not sure worms or spit the ardant yellow corner gray berries
boat

the pace of noise the braiding in motion, braid continuously
a knife song

forget the dark pressing yonder, a train comes inside
squint at self

to break for luck
to hold in the palm for
like consistency what the girls want is stability what sentence
knows how to sit down like that I don't know I get antsy

here's my last idea I won't take up any more time but

worms are just

lips pumped full of spit

you've been kissing a lot as of late or just

you're full of it

that's how you move

fueled by spit, spit slut my friend calls me in my own bedroom

a worm a smile on escape take measure of the canvas and the image bites freedom with a grin, carry on

let the bodies hit the floor

I'm cool with actually I mean actually can we do it actually
yes I'm cool with waiting for the perfect light
and know it won't hold anything at all
I hoped we'd find those clouds brazen against dusk's
rise
actually she told me

we could find phlox nudging the
pine trail, where new bloom pressed my wrist like, can't I
long for surprise

trembled lip unsure, worms and spit, mind the waver as
a gray vibe

actually the translucence of the stems meant I couldn't
look any longer

another broken light
to sit down in luck
to hold in the palm for
like consistency what the girls want is stability what
sentence knows how to sit down like that I don't know I
get antsy

a worm or smile on escape
take measure of the canvas and the image bites freedom
with a grin, carry on
spit slut my friend calls me in my own bedroom,
fueled by spit

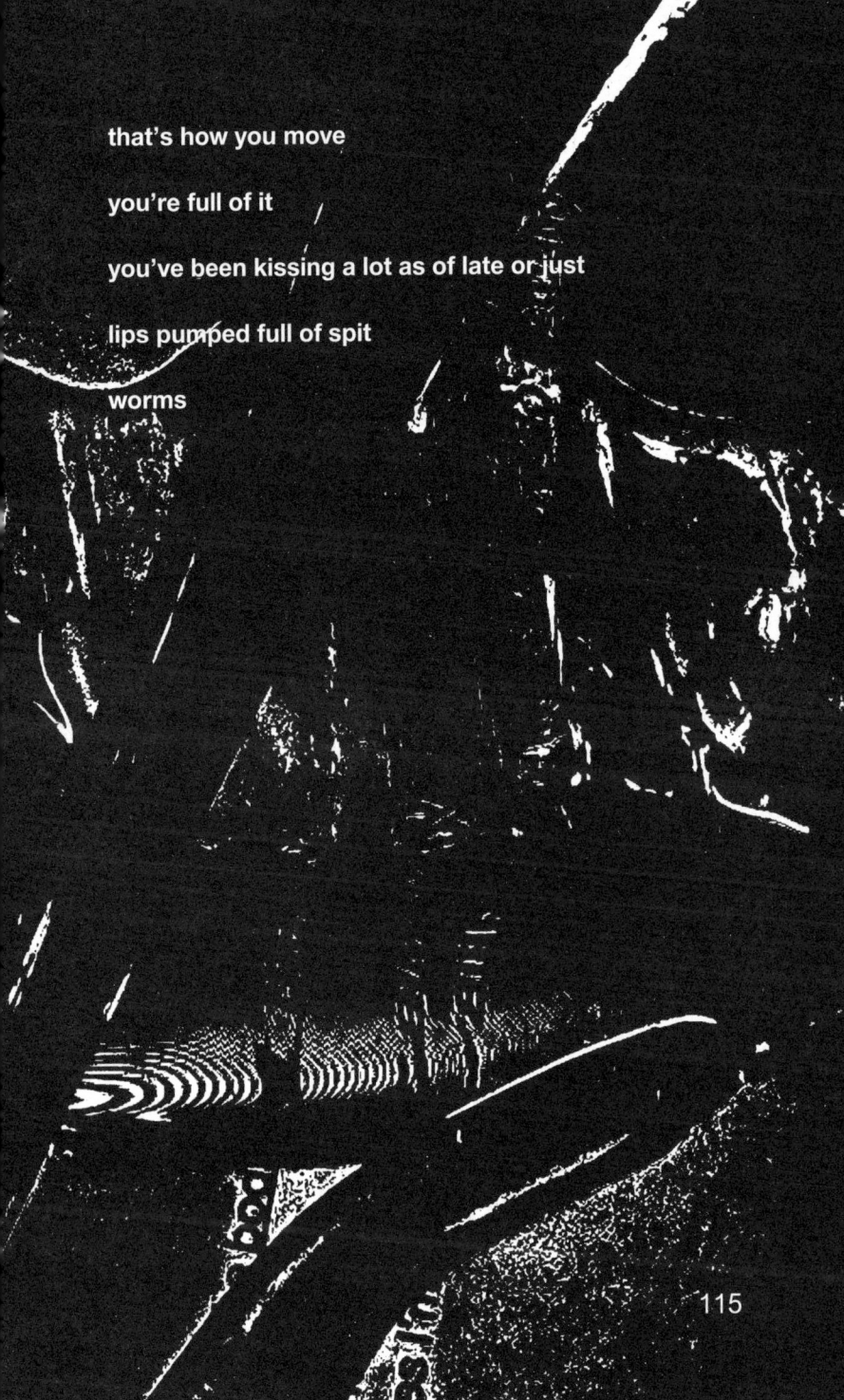

that's how you move

you're full of it

you've been kissing a lot as of late or just

lips pumped full of spit

worms

defragment

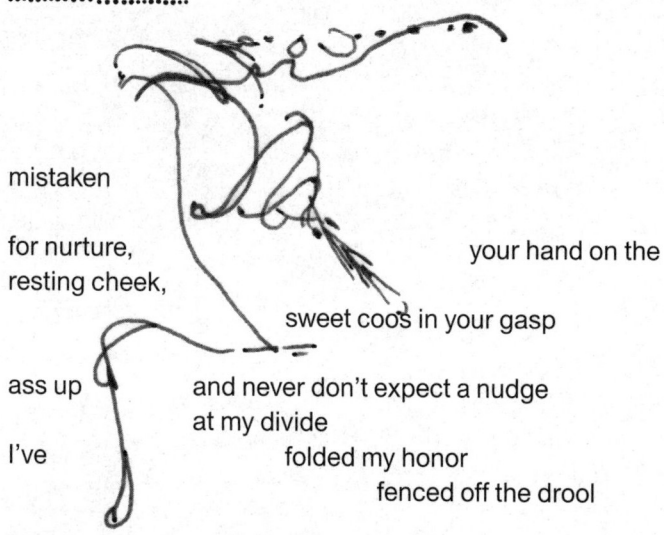

mistaken

for nurture,　　　　　　　　　　　　your hand on the
resting cheek,

　　　　　　　sweet coos in your gasp

ass up　　　and never don't expect a nudge
　　　　　　at my divide
I've　　　　　　folded my honor
　　　　　　　　　fenced off the drool

miraculous the cogent ferment
of your
coddled wet by my thighs

unwrap three caramels
and expose yourself
to the
nascent eros of glue

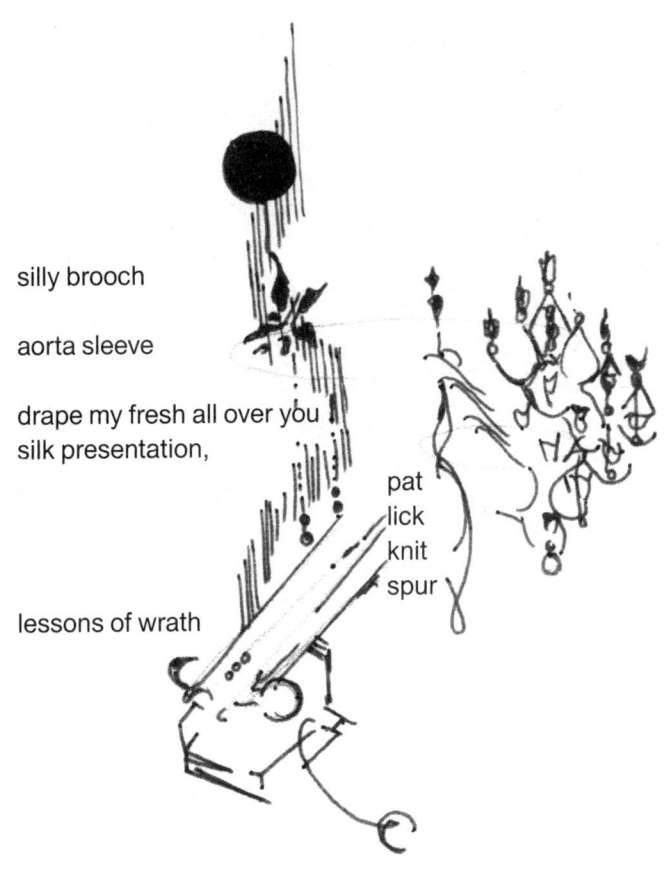

silly brooch

aorta sleeve

drape my fresh all over you
silk presentation,

pat
lick
knit
spur

lessons of wrath

defragment

in costume of care, your hand on the top edge,
swimmy murmur

ass up I'm patient
you butterfly me
I ventriloquize
cage my stream

miraculous the stunning ferment
of your
coddled wet by my thighs

address your fossil
annealing release

fumbling loop
porous valve
draped anew upon you

        throw
        waltz
        knot
        follow

find your devastation in the dew drop

the tips of my ears cat cow
like done done done done
but un wanting for end my hips hop full circle

you're pulsing you're promising

It was a purple night

I'm raising my palms up slowly, drag wax across my vision
Start to stay as moss
Loosen

J turns to me, caught, like I didn't just see her doing that
gazing with a pang
The leather clings to her taut torso as mercury
It's bubble gum, the want to touch her
and the lines of music squiggle vertical blood   un the
veins of her muscles

look how hard I'm into you

  is it just music

  what this produces

Frog begs me, a lesion croons me, nudges crush change
  light touch upon me
        forgotten pawn
puff pinched the image from afar

platform for the map on the palm

toes stick out for cold air

what hint of herbal flavor
merguez
nascent edit
forgiven by pollen
crumbs of a spring afternoon
cruel to leave the moment as ash
a cautionary tail,
                leave something behind
  make waves to trace that that could look more curious
to have it and then to belt it
with patterned stars

ample bell
impeccable shadow
ice edges
    blue image of hints, suggestions
  not of anything that should, but anything that could
        a ray of surmise, puddle dragged by purpose
            caution, where is caution, woken under
melody, creeping cactus
rooted thorns, the bottom blanket
the stained sheet,   thanked that mist pool with   direct
contact

fingers rinsed twice and positioned to weave new forces
upon the day

ice made that last step spell glamour

wet thought
shape sound
lullaby, candelabra, abruptly sprouted brassicas
arms open to test my wingspan
  actual vessel in votive
carve place
apple sardonic attitude.   the more ample this bruise the
melancholy steps mark fruited murmurs   of want and loss
     lark soars knowingly over the picture
       catch place and render it ochre
   woven tightly, only one reigns
                     you will be better off
                        when they leave

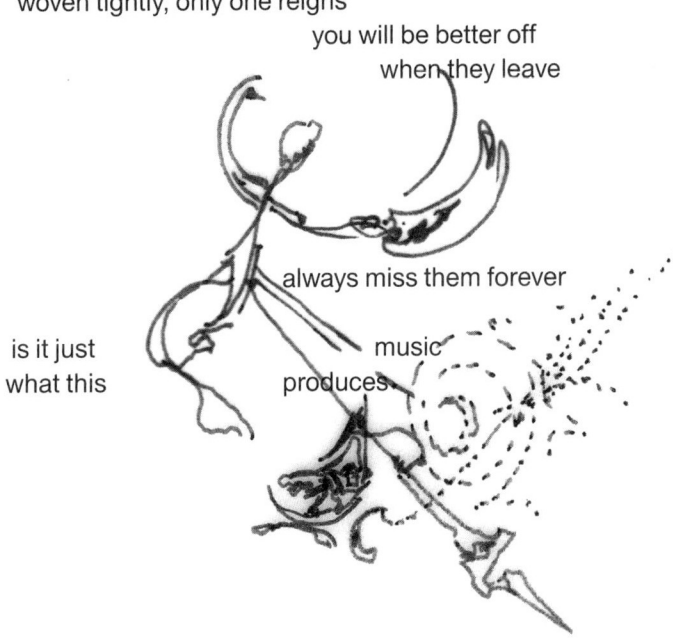

             always miss them forever

is it just   music
what this   produces

razor button

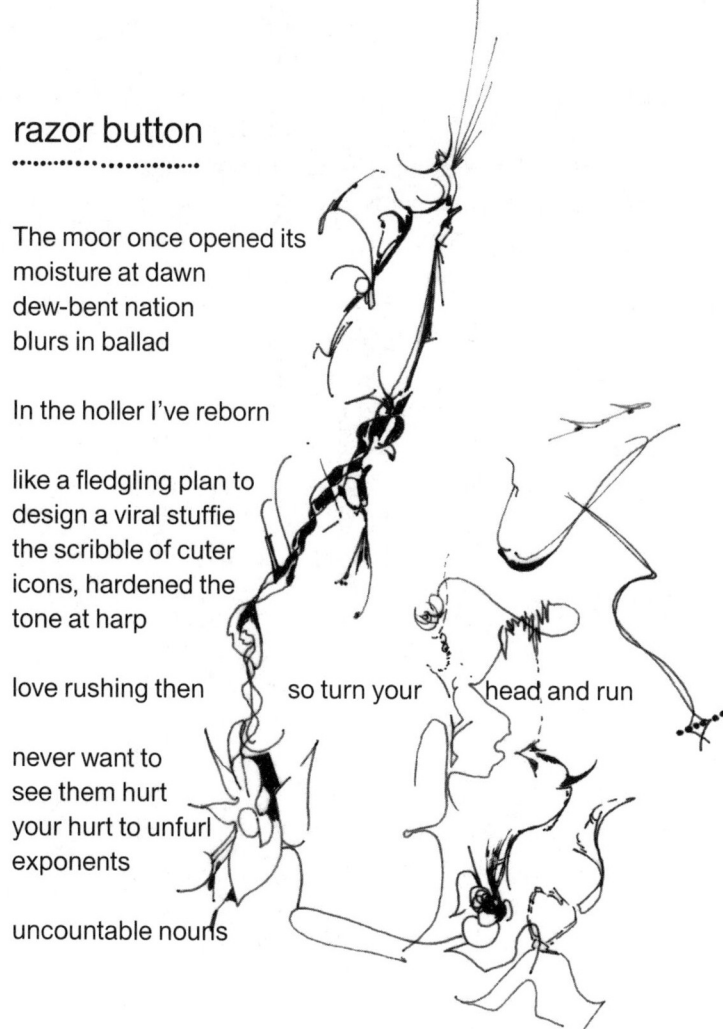

The moor once opened its
moisture at dawn
dew-bent nation
blurs in ballad

In the holler I've reborn

like a fledgling plan to
design a viral stuffie
the scribble of cuter
icons, hardened the
tone at harp

love rushing then   so turn your   head and run

never want to
see them hurt
your hurt to unfurl
exponents

uncountable nouns

my trans not a shape but motion

braided glass

missed you after the volume of faith
filled the speaker and bares a soul
all fours, tumble

twisted glass

dart of haste

ran through form
keep the screen grease smudge
match the filthy history of my bed

some pause some smell yawn the pupil with this, implicit

(the ink enflamed
the imprint of puncture in my gorge
a clot of convulsed purpose
the fascia's gaze locked on itself to
splinter the haptic spark of tissue)

life so sick and beautiful drips with sweat

fang that edgeless candle

simple conversations on the dance floor
strategic so as to handle it
simply checking in with respect
and safety and literal vibes

razor button

the bog released its
wetness at dawn
found the song detached
smudged notes of dew

in the valley I bloom

love rushes past what you're present for

what if
pain without hurt

please

pain without hurt

I'll precisely continue

bolt of pace

run through run past form
leave it honest keep the dirt at the edge

look directly
look precise

precise puncture attach itself to me as imprint
a script drawn with heat for ink

streak the sky

my god's creatures

doing it rn out loud

it's freaky it's calm it's a lantern on wheels and
a slanted floor forever

never saw the vent until now I spit the rest of what I've
fucked left in there
match currents

water spines
like a horror
lips upturn
gape like ran horse
wind-down toys
kite of
pain stars the
core

then maybe
a takeover
or the stitches
clench pearl

another sun
rests
backstage

streak the sky

my god's creatures

all around and vibing

it's freaky it's calm the

stitches clench pearl
kite of
pain stars the
core

another sun rests backstage

Orange peel here

Forget me not

Original speak

Missing dare

Cut the tree into ribs

Collide the strands in flight

Chess eyes

Pompous to think you could name a star

Fermented the community

Betray magic

Answer time

Love by inhalation

Pretend the danger snaps to grid, believe linear

Roll, jump, dream . . . like the machine is equal

like the Wand is the form for the Want

04/23/2022   7:03 am

make pigeons of your truth
if forging this hole
I'll fill you with what I can give
at least light
at best force

cracked the ancient code of this plane
the very angle
the missing tooth
the hood of the car flies up
just before Verazzano
my form a video game

it could happen again
it could happen all at once
my vision
my opal, swirled colored smoke from the egg

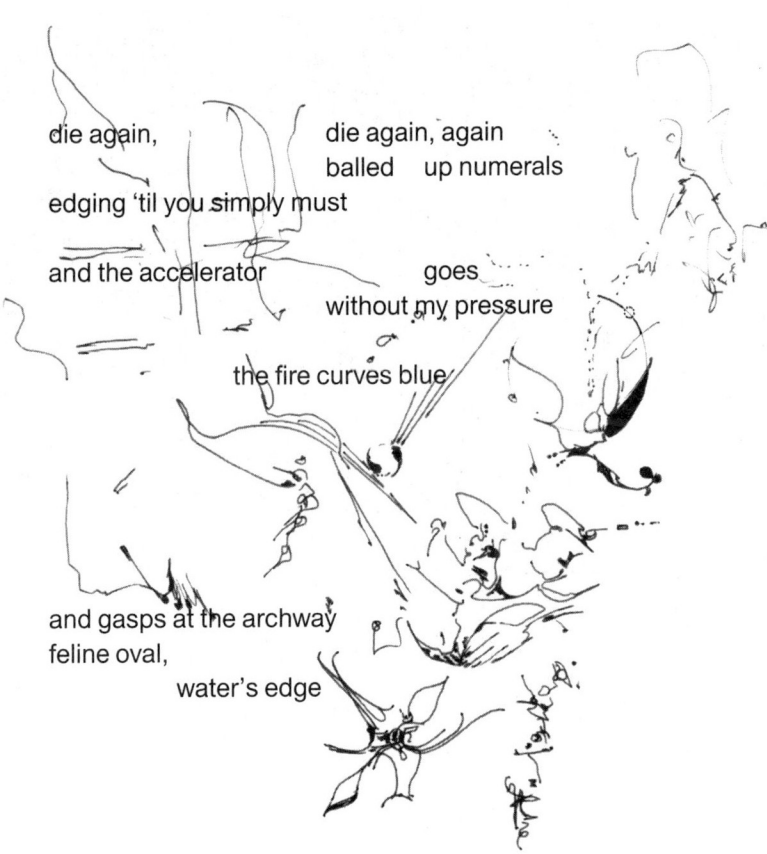

die again,   die again, again
              balled   up numerals
edging 'til you simply must

and the accelerator   goes
                  without my pressure

        the fire curves blue

and gasps at the archway
feline oval,
        water's edge

04/23/2022_____7:03AM

make fowl of your truth
if masking this void
I'll fill you with what I can give
at least salt
at best glue

leak the mystic scripture of this lev
specific measure
the last piece
my windshield a haunting
my frame of sight infected
I figure a distance

could happen again
could happen at any moment
corrupt visions
my opal, colored smoke swirls from the egg
it dies again, dies again, again
dividing the answer
let it go in cacaphony
one light touch

the fire swallows the arch
pierced water tails
comes to reach space

rhapsodomy

bell
bitter greens   forked tongue says

twin statements
and identifies my
other half
or part
like hair can't middle
at all lines
my folded auburn chair
my phantom thrust
I hope you will
I hope you'll will my
overtaking, and pool it into been
haven taken, grant ghouls this present
and
mirrored past
a table makes mention of eden
in all its luxurities/indulgences
and the moment is bitten, the
forbidden pear
scroll in to the next heart
unwind the stairs of god

gauze and feathers
wail dargence as I
spark behance

a skin of wilter
arc fly
oh mist of cause

looking   around
myself

what if I were to start like
"As a transsexual"
"As a votive candle"
I blink heat as it bloods
your curiosity

I drip slowly, just to make certain
the wave rolled dice, fasts for luck,
cushion beauty's gore of devastation

rhapsodomy

bell
bitter greens   forked tongue says

twin statements
and identifies my
other half
or part
like hair can't middle
at all lines
my folded auburn chair
my phantom thrust
I hope you will
I hope you'll will my
overtaking, and pool it into been
haven taken, grant ghouls this present
and
mirrored past
a table makes mention of Eden
in all its luxuries/indulgences
and the moment is bitten, the
forbidden pear
scroll into the next heart
unwind the stairs of god

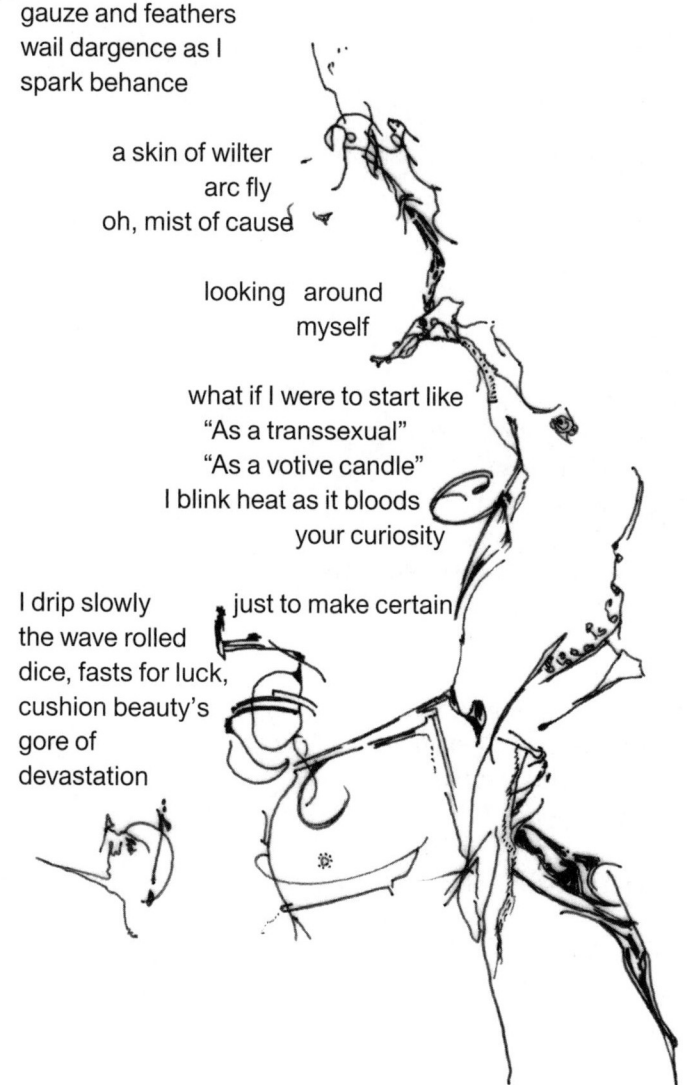

gauze and feathers
wail dargence as I
spark behance

      a skin of wilter
         arc fly
   oh, mist of cause

        looking   around
              myself

     what if I were to start like
      "As a transsexual"
      "As a votive candle"
  I blink heat as it bloods
        your curiosity

I drip slowly   just to make certain
the wave rolled
dice, fasts for luck,
cushion beauty's
gore of
devastation

itselfs

a sphere wrung out finds itself a wave
mirrored floor slowly hush becomes carpet become moss
lasso the clock face a ferris wheel

I told you so

the spiral deep throats the pen

simple pain   gasping daiquiri   trust—
frozen or on the rocks?

tin shell   damp choice   this one this one   slides shut

shallow dust I couldn't catch
bent across the opal's distance

come pull on questions
hold strings
loosen rust wrinkle melody

snail in the pocket
Find ovals   encase the birthed in blight

Allegro *bends* Adagio *ascends* Concerto *swims* Chant
delineates Bass *gestures* Andante *engorges* Chorus
candies Air *flounders* Arrangement *mounts* Cantata *over*

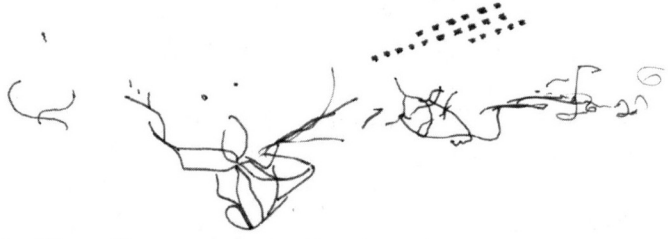

brriiiiing riiii nnnnnn gggggGhgghgg ri ng

in portions the swell swims to nurture
scratches in wet clay

If beauty is in the whistle, blood is a day

score:
fountain glimmer *shhh* oak fixation
 fascia.

laughter in the saxophone
belays mischief

the web is red neon is pipes of lava
circles announce collision with a sway
slow, knowing nod to
forgive the When and spin worms upon the treble

Something in
the ridden moan

in tempered begging
melody pleasing
return to the mouth and resist once more

itselfs

a gnaw wrung out finds itself a confession
the wall grows lights slowly sighs becomes a wash
each number falls down from the circle

the spiral deep-throats the pen

you told me so

rust melody
freeze trust and unlock ovals

Harmony *bites* Vibrato *flosses* Aria *belays* Tanpura *curdles*
Rasa *teases* Raga *watches* Arabesque *slices*

mmmmmmmMMMMmmmMMMMmmMM!

beauty is in the split of wind

laughter in the saxophone

score: carpet   shallow   *ahhh* clay   pocket   fascia.

Something in
the ridden moan
in tempered begging
return to the mouth and clench the bell

copy your spell

trenchant reduction, analogous brush—
jinx box—stiff, nothing of waver sits in the parting
To shy from concretion

swan song
so long
godspeed

had to know
that
nothing orates water   suspense   elsewhere,
pliable trace,
        imagine wire wailing,

another steel window,   to lake my inside, is
another body pliable?

I was a   sample, a paradigm   nodding
near clues. I was   genetically   pistillate
     though this was in vain.   Whose voids are
these, in plea. Else plunges into   the when and hugs itself,
won't come out.

     Here is the null in pose. A rouse in the air
                               of the other.

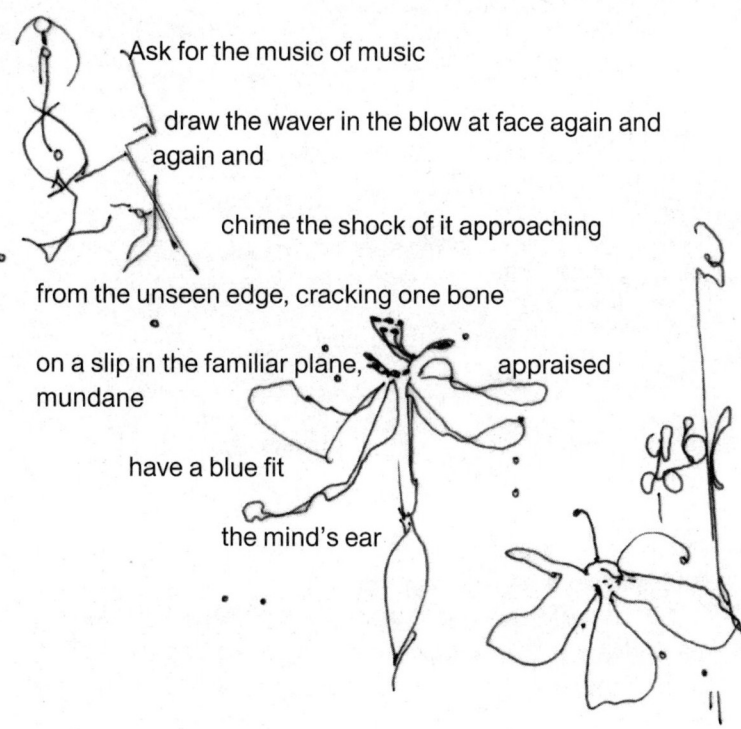

Ask for the music of music

draw the waver in the blow at face again and again and

chime the shock of it approaching

from the unseen edge, cracking one bone

on a slip in the familiar plane, appraised mundane

have a blue fit

the mind's ear

copy your spell

callous miniature, parallel pen, charm lock ⌐   set,
not one quiver at division
I shy from concretion

winged hymn,
come through
and take off

I don't know does
wind express water?   if it leaves, waves in trace
this step strikes another, imagine the fence walking,
another vined page, to rain
my circulation, is a further body possible?

I was a loosened present, a pattern evading the clue
my center void of pollen, no anther, no filament, but ok
let's scar the cursor. Whose voids are these, in plea.
There and this run from now.

Ask for the love of love

paint the falter, ring its arrival

Is there an object?

crack the bones of the familiar plane, scrunch it

take on a bluer fit

the mind's Here

gave me nothing to answer
••

truth in the netted connection of velcro,   trip what lusher look, rip and parse faith

tongue makes loose claims.

on conditions of hydration and nebula of the day,

belief that vibrates at second sight of my outstretched palms,　　　　locus behind, eyes in a pulley cycle of coaxing,　　　　　the strings of dusk visible in pluck by the other senses,

something mistaken for something, there's a wobble in the moon's orbit,
　　　　don't wanna move on let it all come in
take me in　　　　　　as though you'd chew the seeds before hesitance.
encircling bolt.

butterfly the eclipse.　　cunt flexible tract. signal a likely
structure.　　　　　　　insist you consider this moment
once more,　　　　　　at a later time.
Order the color and passion, a rasa unique to the raga in
question.　　　　　　　delude me better. honey do not
forget do not forget play the moment as a freed engraving,

skate webs of needles on euphony

they could say

the risk of your eye-laden mouth the fluke of your drifting
thigh
more alluring more exquisite than　　　　　　　　　　a
potent thunder giving sigh to rigid rock.

the observers at a loss in midst of sharpened petals . . .
their mother's song nudged into improper hands.

or was there the wrong vegetable at the one stand.

someone with ears for it I want to know the little ones can
counter.
　　　　　　crash sills of mixing and gift shop
and massage division's very first bend.

awash
with my wrist at your chin,   nudge
your sight to my lips part on you,

away from my fingers, stained sun by daal and rice,
been dangling the same kind of exigent wonder

 in the wash of pollen,   in suckling the warming spices,
alium sweat and slip around the corner of coy
          behind the knee,   a slicked lust
column,

 my hands make mouthfuls, grains of rice, slightly lower
head sideways,
the spoon pouts for attention

with much exuberance the pain
 a close light
runs   to the joy

sound the buttered bell a jagged peal
feet   in and out like   the ground is hot and
exciting or   are you supposed to hear this
too curious to clip motion

can't bear to couldn't bear to won't bear not to

It lands because its charge and reactivity are similar to those of the halogens. Due to the instability, they smell us like friction-sensitive explosives. The best known can be formed from silver and lust, dissolved in pictures and reacted with fervor. The weak and label-driven bond is responsible for their instability. Some like this very easily form a stable triple bond to another compound, a stumbling grip at the core of the cloud.

ecology of alias as arias and

rushed flesh
all the sand of mutter

pined for a pinch

gig
 gle game

match on the left side and
missing from the sight side

my frightened pleasure
the animals go for daily fittings in blue water

I'm cool with it complete supposing I'm cool with the air
putting us in sight   in the meantime one maybe
won't be able to keep ledge of it at all

yet wished to glimpse the raving clouds at their last supple dance,

actually she said   we might find the chanterelles
closer to the made road

where esurience rushes my tiptoes

make spores of awe

to measure our sonance

slid fury   the mostly   comma the caution
 the shall shaping   sordid

stick pulse

a forgive me light
if

we could purse sweat : bait landscape : make miniature
sanctity

sad carcass in sarcasm
other mirth dampened
tools to spin spit like it could share itself as fabric

sardonic surprise, lattice face, mistake membrane,
 truth plume, eager to stumble, diving off the edge a bit . . .

the
new doja
is   wavy is bumpin is making me want to dance in a
space   simply see each other happy

is making me swoon tears
at every regular shake of branches in the sky

sym a sphere cornered by
hungering proteins washing time

bloom type speak
myriad encounters at the bud
actually could thicken the tale and
hold my hands behind my back really expecting to feel
something
there a lace of fur   a lace-up of fur and muscle

enlightenmentally stable
I refuse a definable state

rekindle as plastic carnage, mirror rust

Acknowledgments

I am grateful that this book finds a home with Wendy's Subway. Thank you for the opportunity to share this work, for supporting its form through many stages, for your fostering and patience in the process. Thank you to my editors Corinne Butta and Rachel Valinsky, thank you to my dear friend Sunny Iyer. Making this book has been very important to me.

Thank you to Mónica de la Torre for your close read of this book, for encouraging me to push the form and write a second version of each poem, and for telling me to allow myself to merge my languages of drawing and writing.

Thank you to Noah Ross and *baest journal*, and Sophie Whitmore from Hi-Lo Press, where a couple of these poems have appeared before.

Thank you to Dawn Lundy Martin, whom I had the pleasure of working alongside to teach her class, "Risk and the Art of Poetry." I was encouraged by a sturdy grace of mentorship and was able to confront my language in dialogue with the students. I was in awe of the students' care for the world and their work, for each others' values.

Thank you to my teachers at Bard for your guidance, critique, references, and attention. Thank you Cedar Sigo, Christopher Rey Pérez, CAConrad, Taylor Davis, Laura Huertas Millán, Lotus L. Kang, Mirene Arsanios, Sara Magenheimer, Michael Bell-Smith, Ariel Goldberg, Julian Talamantez Brolaski.

Thank you to Bianca Rae Messinger and Zoey Lubitz, who have lovingly encouraged my writing over the last decade.

I want to thank friends who have inspired, read, challenged, and listened to my work; friends who inspire the ways I love, fight, fail, and grow; and who I get to share these gifts with—Nora Treatbaby, Carolyn Ferrucci, Drew Zeiba, Funto Omojola, Emir West, Syd Yocom, Matia Emsellem, Ricky Sallay Zoker, Tamara Santibañez, Miya Shaffer, Willa Nasatir, Daniel Perlmutter, Ethan Skaates, Sarina Hahn.

These are love poems, and while their first versions were written a couple years ago, these loves continue to move through new shapes. I am so grateful for the ways that the relationships in my life have surprised me in shifted arrangements.

I am so lucky for the care and brilliance of my friend Rissa Hochberger in making this book together. Thank you for your deep intention to understand my language of vision, and for your grace moving through this process. You are family to me. It is a blessing to have life together. I look forward to the ways we will grow in collaboration. Thank you for seeing with me.

Cursive Paradise
© 2025 Kaur Alia Ahmed

All rights reserved. No part of this book may be used or reproduced without prior permission of the publisher.

Passage Series
First Edition, 2025
Edition of 1,000 copies
ISBN: 979-8-9909878-2-1
LCCN: 2024941556

Edited by Corinne Butta
Proofread by Rachel Valinsky
Designed by Rissa Hochberger
Typeset in Union
Printed at KOPA, Lithuania

Published by Wendy's Subway
379 Bushwick Avenue
Brooklyn, NY 11206
wendyssubway.com

Wendy's Subway is a nonprofit reading room, writing space, and independent publisher located in Brooklyn.

The authorized representative in the EU for product safety and compliance is eucomply OÜ, Pärnu mnt 139b-14, 11317 Tallinn, Estonia, hello@eucompliancepartner.com, +33757690241. Our official distribution partner is Antenne books ltd.

The Passage Series features titles by emerging writers and artists whose work manifests in innovative, hybrid, and cross-genre forms that imagine new possibilities and expressions of the poetic, the political, and the social

Cursive Paradise was selected as the 2021 Carolyn Bush Award recipient.

The Passage Series is supported, in part, by the New York State Council on the Arts with support of the Office of the Governor and the New York State Legislature, and public funds funds from the New York City Department of Cultural Affairs in Partnership with the City Council.